REAR ADMIRAL EDWIN T. LAYTON
UNITED STATES NAVY, RETIRED

Edwin Thomas Layton was born in Nauvoo, Illinois, on April 7, 1903, son of George Ellis and Mary Catherine (Fulton) Layton. After graduation from the Galesburg High School in 1920, he entered the U. S. Naval Academy on appointment from the Fifteenth District of the State of Illinois. Graduated and commissioned Ensign in June 1924, he subsequently progressed in grade, attaining that of Captain, to date from June 1, 1943. His selection for the rank of Rear Admiral was approved by the President on July 24, 1953, his date of rank July 1, 1953.

Following graduation from the Naval Academy, he served successively in the USS WEST VIRGINIA and the USS CHASE until June 1929, when he was ordered to duty in the Office of the U. S. Naval Attache at the American Embassy, Tokyo, Japan. Here he was under instruction in the Japanese language until October 1932. The following four months he was Assistant Naval Attache at the American Legation, Peiping, China.

In February 1933 he returned to the United States and served in the Office of Naval Intelligence, Navy Department, Washington, D. C., until June 1933. Then he joined the USS PENNSYLVANIA, serving in that battleship until June 1936. He received Letters of Commendation from the Secretary of Navy and Commander in Chief, U. S. Fleet, in 1934 and 1935 respectively, for gunnery excellence and special performance in Fleet Problem XVI.

He returned to the Office of Naval Intelligence, Navy Department, where he remained on duty until February 1937, after which from April of that year to March 1939 he served as Assistant Naval Attache to Japan, attached to the American Embassy, Tokyo. In April 1939 he assumed command of the USS BOGGS and served while that destroyer operated with Mobile Target Division ONE, Base Force, until December 1940. He then reported for duty on the staff of the Commander in Chief, U. S. Fleet, and in February 1941 was transferred to duty on the staff of the Commander in Chief, Pacific Fleet. Serving as Combat Intelligence Officer on the staff, Fleet Admiral Chester W. Nimitz, USN, he was present with him when the Japanese formally surrendered aboard the USS MISSOURI in Tokyo Bay on September 2, 1945 (EST).

He was awarded the Distinguished Service Medal "For exceptionally meritorious service to the Government of the United States...as Officer in Charge of all Intelligence in the Pacific Ocean Area and subsequently as Pacific Fleet Combat Intelligence Officer, December 1941 to September 1945...." The citation states that he "analyzed and precisely evaluated the capabilities and intentions of the enemy's air, sea and ground forces...(and) rendered invaluable assistance to the Pacific Fleet and all commands of the Pacific Ocean areas in planning and conducting every amphibious campaign, Fleet engatement and Carrier attack. His timely and accurate intelligence information, vital to the security of our fighting forces and essential to their successful operations, contributed inestimably to our victory over the enemy..."

R. Adm. S. T. Layton, USN, Ret.   Page 2

   Detached from the Pacific Fleet in February 1945, he returned to the United States, and from April of that year to August 1948 commanded the U. S. Naval Net Depot, at Tiburon, California. He returned to Washington in October 1948 to serve until May 1950 as Director of the U. S. Navy School, Naval Intelligence. For six months thereafter he served as District Intelligence Officer on the staff of the Commandant, Fourteenth Naval District, Headquarters in Pearl Harbor, Territory of Hawaii. During this time he served additionally as Force Intelligence Officer, Commander Naval Forces Far East, from July through September 1950.

   He received a Letter of Commendation from Commander Naval Forces Far East, which states in part: "During the initial stages of the Korean War, 8 July to 18 September 1950, he developed and guided an intelligence organization for Commander Naval Forces Far East, that provided the Commander with capabilities to effectively meet newly imposed responsibilities and to evaluate obscure military situations quickly, affording thereby the clearest interpretation of existing problems...."

   From January 1951 to June 1953 he served as Fleet Intelligence Officer on the staff of Commander in Chief, U. S. Pacific Fleet, and as Assistant Chief of Staff for Joint Intelligence, Joint Staff, Commander in Chief, Pacific. In July 1953 he was assigned to the Office of the Joint Chiefs of Staff, Washington, D. C., as Assistant Director, Joint Staff for Intelligence, and on August 17, 1954, he was designated Deputy Director for Intelligence, Joint Chiefs of Staff. He was Assistant Chief of Staff to the Commander in Chief, U. S. Pacific Fleet from September 1956 until April 1958, when he assumed duty as Director of the Naval Intelligence School at the Naval Receiving Station, Washington, D. C. He remained there until relieved of all active duty pending his retirement, effective November 1, 1959.

   In addition to the Distinguished Service Medal and Commendation Ribbon, Rear Admiral Layton has the Ribbon for the Navy Unit Commendation; the American Defense Service Medal, Fleet Clasp; the Asiatic-Pacific Campaign Medal; the World War II Victory Medal; the National Defense Service Medal; the Korean Service Medal; and the United Nations Service Medal.

   He and his wife, the former Dagne Solveig Wickstrom of Duluty, Minnesota, have two children, Daniel Earle and Carol Anne Layton.

NAVY - Office of Information
Biographies Branch
9 December 1959

DECLARATION OF TRUST

The undersigned does hereby appoint and designate as his Trustee herein, the Secretary-Treasurer and Publisher of the United States Naval Institute to perform and discharge the following duties, powers, and privileges in connection with the possession and use of a certain taped interview between the undersigned and the Oral History Department of the United States Naval Institute.

1. Classification of Transcript

   (a) The original tape recordings made in May 1970 and the original transcript made from such recordings are classified CLOSED until ten (10) years hence, or on the death of the interviewee, which ever occurs first.

   (b) The revised, edited and corrected version of the original transcript has been made by the interviewee and forwarded to the Oral History Department of the United States Naval Institute in May 1972. This revised, edited and corrected manuscript is classified PERMISSION REQUIRED, and permission must be obtained in writing from the interviewee before this revised, edited and corrected interview can be examined, as well as prior to quoting or citing such revised, edited and corrected interview.

   (c) Copies of the above revised, edited and corrected version of the original transcript may, subject to conditions set forth above, be furnished to the Office of Naval History, the U.S. Naval Academy Library and the U.S. Naval War College (custody of the Edwin T. Layton Military Chair of Intelligence).

It is expressly understood that in giving this authorization, I am in no way precluded from placing such restrictions as I may desire upon use of the interview at any time during my lifetime, nor does this authorization in any way affect my rights to the copyright of my literary expressions that may be contained in the interview.

WITNESS my hand and seal this _____ day of _____, 1972.

_____
EDWIN T. LAYTON
Rear Admiral, USN (Retired)

I hereby accept and consent to the foregoing Declaration of Trust and the powers therein conferred upon me as Trustee:

Layton #1 - 1

Interview #1

Rear Admiral Edwin T. Layton, U.S. Navy (Ret.)

Subject: Biography   Date: May 30, 1970

Interviewer: Etta-Belle Kitchen, CDR, USN (Ret.)

Q: This is interview #1 with Rear Admiral Edwin T. Layton at his home "Landfall" Route 1, 10 Malpaso Road in Carmel, California. This is May 30, 1970 and I'm awfully happy to have this opportunity to speak with you, Admiral.

Admiral, since this is your biography and we want to talk with you at length concerning your career, I want to comment on your birthplace which was Nauvoo, Illinois.

Layton: That's right.

Q: My recollection of history is that the Mormons settled there, did they not, on their way, their trip to Utah?

Layton: They settled there and then they were driven out and left there for Utah. They were driven out by almost a civil war.

Q: Do you have any recollections of those days?

Layton: They were before my time.

Q: They were way before your time but the question I had was whether there were any early incidents in your bringing up or items which you think might have had an effect on your character or your personality.

Layton: I think the location did. You see, it was on the Mississippi River. That's why the Mormons chose it; it was on a bluff, at a bend of the river, the Mississippi River flowing to the north, west, and south of the town. It was my earliest association with water. I remember the Mississippi River steamboats and the life on the river. I don't claim to be a "Mark Twain" but I was very impressed with the Mississippi River, and the people who worked there. I was impressed, too, with the Mormons because they had chosen this place which had been shunned before because of the swamps. The swamps bred mosquitoes and the mosquitoes carried malaria, so people hadn't settled there. If they did, they left. The Mormons, being enterprising, drained the swamps, and recovered valuable garden plots and agricultural land, which brought more people there; this made the Mormons more prosperous until their policies, particularly those regarding plural marriage, aroused the people in the neighborhood.

Now when I lived there the old Mormon houses still stood and were still occupied. They were rather handsome in a simple way. I'm not a Mormon. The Mormons would come back to Nauvoo each year for a kind of a camp meeting which was normally held in the city square. Of course, you'd see this as a young fellow and you got to know some of the Mormon boys and some of the younger girls and play games together.

Q: As it happens, I was raised in a Mormon community myself and all of the areas, I'm sure affect one's personality and one's character.

Layton: I think it's taught me a bit of tolerance of the other man's view; I had been told as a child that Mormons had horns and were real "devils with a forked tail". Then to see that they were really honest human beings, you learn not to trust everything you're told.

Q: True. And your life in the future, you have much association with people of varying races and undoubtedly this has helped in having you tolerant toward them. Does the fact that you were raised on the Mississippi indicate why you were inclined toward the Navy life?

Layton: I think so. From childhood, I had intended to go to the Naval Academy.

Q: Well, why had you always intended to go to the Naval Academy? Can you identify the reason?

Layton: I was interested in going to sea; the Mississippi River may have influenced my thoughts, I don't know.

Layton #1 - 4

Q: I think it's interesting now in retirement, I want to put on the record that you are living by the sea and you have a most magnificent view from your front window.

Layton: Well, my wife and I have always wanted to find a view of the sea, if we could, when we settled down.

Q: Certainly it is a beautiful spot. Do you have any recollections of your Academy days that you think we could put on the record?

Layton: None particularly that I recall. They were just average days, no particular outstanding events that I recall.

Q: Do you remember any of your classmates who were particularly noteworthy.

Layton: No.

Q: Then when you graduated in 1924 your first two duties were on the West Virginia and the Chase.

Layton: The West Virginia was a new ship, going on a shakedown cruise to Europe. The shakedown cruise was cut short -- part of the original itinerary which included a cruise into the Mediterranean (Italy, North Africa, Greece and Gibralter) was cancelled. We learned that this was because of increased tension with Japan at that time -- 1924. Our studies of naval history at the Naval Academy, plus the uproar over exclusion of Japanese immigration to the U.S. and the recent Washington disarmament conference of 1922 still fresh in our recollection, focused our attention on Japan at that time. Because of the increased tension between Japan and the U.S., we were to expedite a curtailed shakedown cruise and make preparations to join the Fleet, which we did in October of that year. Therefore, I began studying news reports and reading about Japan, with a little more interest.

Q: When were you detached from the West Virginia?

Layton: The following April, I believe. It was before the cruise to Australia. I was detached in Honolulu, went out to Pearl Harbor and joined the destroyer Chase (323) which left the next morning to go back to Mare Island Navy Yard for an overhaul. I liked destroyer life very much; we went to Australia from the Navy Yard via Pearl Harbor again, with only for a brief stopover for fuel and provisions.

The Australian cruise was very interesting and destroyer life absorbing; junior officers who on a battleship had little responsibility were given full responsibilities on a destroyer, since only six officers including the Commanding officer, were assigned.

Q: What was your duty on this destroyer?

Layton #1 - 6

Layton: Watch officer, Torpedo officer, and First Lieutenant, Assistant Gunnery Officer, Stores Officer and Commissary Officer.

Q: You had your hands full then.

Layton: Well, everyone did. It's odd to recall that in the Chase (323) there was only one chief yeoman and two yeoman strikers. A small ship had practically the same number of reports (engineering, navigational, gunnery, supply, personnel reports, etc.) that a large ship had but they could be done by one yeoman and two strikers, while a large ship required some 30 or 40 yeomen for these. This was an indication of the paperwork and bureaucracy that we've accumulated.

Q: Do you remember any incidents in Australia?

Layton: None of importance, no.

Q: Who was the skipper of the Chase?

Layton: His name was Allen G. Olsen. He was a pleasant skipper; he wasn't what one would call a "sun-downer" nor a "driver". He was a more easy-going type and very pleasant.

Q: Who were some of your other shipmates?

Layton: We had two who also became admirals. One was Roland

Layton #1 - 7

Smoot, later on Assistant Chief of Naval Personnel; the other was Carl Espe, later Director of Naval Intelligence.

Q: That was a handy friendship to make, wasn't it?

Layton: Well, I guess it was. I never thought of it that way. One other officer on the Chase that was outstanding was Lieutenant Joseph Severens, the Executive Officer. Later on he went into lighter-than-air and was on board the Akron when it was lost off the East Coast, and was killed. He was one of the finest naval officers and an inspiring leader.

Q: What rank was he?

Layton: Lieutenant.

Q: He was a Lieutenant and you were an Ensign at the time.

Layton: Yes. One event on the West Virginia had a considerable influence on my life. As I said, the West Virginia arrived on the West Coast to join the Fleet on Navy Day, October 27th, 1924. On January 3rd or 4th 1925, the West Virginia, her sister ship the Colorado and another new ship, the Tennessee, I believe it was, were sent to San Francisco to be the host ships for the Japanese Midshipmen's Training Squadron, the three old armored cruisers the Asama, the Yakumo, and the Idzumo. Each of the most junior ensigns of each of our three ships were told off to be the opposite number and escort of a Japanese midshipman. These Japanese midshipmen had completed their course of instruction at Etajima and were taking their final cruise (actually their only cruise) upon the completion of which they would be commissioned as an Ensign. I was made the boarding officer, and also acted as the representative of the West Virginia's junior officers' mess in making the boarding call on our "opposite number", the Asama. I found the Japanese very eager to be friendly and, surprisingly, fine young men.

Q: Why do you say "surprisingly"?

Layton: Yes; I was surprised that they spoke such good English. Half of them spoke perfect English. The other half spoke excellent French. My friends who had taken French said that the Japanese midshipmen spoke colloquial Parisian French of the kind that we didn't learn at our Naval Academy. The Japanese who had taken English -- there were only two foreign languages for them, English or French -- spoke colloquial English of the finest quality and could converse with ease, and fluency. But here is the real kicker -- there wasn't one single U.S. official -- no Naval officer, or anyone on our side, who could speak one word of Japanese! For the first time I learned what "losing face" was. I felt ashamed for the United States, feeling that we should have had someone there who could speak Japanese, too. I was with my "opposite number", this midshipman, day after day. We went to all kinds of receptions and official parties. Our ship's boats could leave our ship, go in via our opposite number ship, pick up our "opposite numbers" to go ashore. We'd be their guide and escorts and see to it that they got to the place on time and then get them back at the proper time unless they wanted to go sightseeing or shopping, when you'd offer to help them. We had lots of fun. As a matter of fact, my opposite number wanted to visit and see an American speakeasy and night-club, so I took him to both; he had a wonderful time. As a matter of fact, the young ladies that I had asked to accompany us to the night-club were a little reluctant to go out with a "Jap", but they finally consented to go and they had a nice time, too. My opposite number was very impressed and pleased.

Q: Were you in uniform?

Layton: Oh yes, of course.

Q: Both the Japanese and you.

Layton: Yes. After the Japanese ships had left San Francisco I wrote an official letter to the Navy Department pointing out the lack of U.S. officials who could speak Japanese; that I felt that we ought to have had somebody there who could speak Japanese; that if we didn't have such a policy, we should have one; and if they needed a volunteer for someone to learn

Layton #1 - 10

the Japanese language, I would do so.

Q: That was interesting.

Layton: And I got a . . .

Q: I know what happened.

Layton: I got the standard form letter acknowledging receipt of my letter; calling my attention to a paragraph in the Bureau of Navigation manual. I looked up the reference that dealt with foreign language instruction and found that two naval officers each year, and one Marine officer each third year, were sent to Tokyo to study Japanese. I then applied but their reply pointed out their requirements= completion of five years sea duty, be unmarried, have an outstanding record, and be suitably recommended. So I continued to show my continuing interest and at the end of five years sea service I received the assignment. I went from San Francisco to Japan aboard the SS <u>President Adams</u>. On that ship was a Lieutenant Rochefort (and his wife and their young son) who were also going to Tokyo for language study.

Q: Were there any incidents going out on the ship that you recall?

Layton: None that I recall.

Q: Well, you answered one of my questions which was going to be what were the circumstances in which you were assigned to Japan to learn the Japanese language and you have already told me that. Also, in those years, the depression was going on in this country. Were you affected by that at all?

Layton: Not directly. There was also a depression going on in Japan.

Q: There was.

Layton: It was most difficult to be able to live on a junior lieutenant's salary. The Japanese yen was based on gold; two yen for one dollar, and living in Japan was very, very expensive. Taxis were very expensive and one just couldn't afford such a luxury. This helped in your language study since you were forced to get around on street cars, busses or the inter-urban cars, or walk. Walking was good exercise and also helped in making conversation with shop keepers and others.

Q: Rickshaws were available in those days, weren't they?

Layton: A few. They had them for tourists, but there weren't many rickshaws, really. Taxis had come in general use in larger cities like Tokyo and Yokohama. Rickshaws were still in use in small cities and villages.

Q: Did you find it difficult to learn the Japanese language?

Layton: In the beginning, no more so than a child here has in learning English as he grows up, or than a Japanese child has of learning Japanese in Tokyo. You were taught as if you were a child (and it was the right way!) by learning through your ears, through speech, as a child learns through its ears, rather than through books. Books came later. Only after you have acquired a vocabulary and can use it to speak of simple matters, express your wishes, or feelings do you start to read. Mr. Naganuma, our instructor (who had designed the new course that Rochefort and I were taking) had decided that using Japanese primary school texts was the wrong way for a foreigner to learn the language.

His idea was that when children start school, in Japan (or anywhere), they had at that stage already acquired a basic knowledge of their language, conversationally, and could express themselves in simple terms. Since all of his foreign students were adults it was necessary first of all to teach them to speak, enough basic language so they could converse -- make known wants, express their feelings or ideas. Once this was achieved, instruction in reading and writing could be taken up.

Q: It seems sensible to me, too.

Layton: This is the way it now is being taught at the Defense

Language Institute and elsewhere. The U.S. military services "borrowed" Mr. Naganuma's system, including his texts, during World War II when they were training many Japanese linguists.

Q: That's interesting. Did you have any incidents that you recall that were of particular interest to you in Japan that affected you later in your duties?

Layton: When naval language students had finished their first period of closely supervised instruction directly under Mr. Naganuma, they had progressed to the point of being able to read a little, and write a little, and had a good understanding of the grammar and structure of the Japanese language. At this juncture bachelors/students were supposed to move "into the country" - away from Tokyo and English language usage. This surrounded the student with the language, forced him to rely exclusively on his Japanese for 24 hours every day, month after month. This made the student expand his vocabulary and his list of characters and compounds. "In the country", one found an instructor--usually a retired college professor or other teacher for daily lessons and grammar work but also carried out a correspondence; in Japanese with your Tokyo instructor. The latter would send you newspaper articles in Japanese, which you would translate into English and return. These would be corrected or commented on and sent to you along with sample grammatical exercises to correct your mistakes or misinterpretation of a Japanese expression or word usage.

Layton #1 - 14

My "country instructor" was a retired gentleman of culture, a "student of the Chinese Classics" and of Oriental History and Art.

One day he said something that I should have remembered years later: we were discussing Japan, the Japanese, and why they act and think the way they do. He said, "You must never forget the Japanese capacity for revenge." "As you know, "revenge" is the central theme of our drama (the Kabuki theatre), the central theme in much of our history and poetry, in old novels and in today's movie scrips." "Never forget it. It is the strongest motivating influence in our life."

He also said: "Never forget that we Japanese cannot forget, nor forgive the U.S. for having classed us as second-class or third-class citizens when it barred Japanese immigration in 1924, along with (here his face was contorted with hate and with scorn) Indians, Chinese, Koreans--Indonesians and scum like that." He said "Always remember that in the Japanese mind we are a superior race." He added "Being excluded from America was an insult but being included by the U.S. with Koreans, Chinese etc., was a stain on our honor that calls for revenge." I recalled those words when I reached my office in Pearl Harbor at around 8:35 or 8:40 a.m. on 7 December 1941 -- as the Japanese "second wave" attack was in progress - and the Arizona, the Cassin and Downs were exploding.

In discussions with me he was most candid! I was most interested in why Japanese do certain things the way they do-- why they think the way they do--why they approach a problem the way they do. He would try to show the basic reasoning of Japanese thought processes, and cite historical and cultural examples to illustrate motivation, logic, or custom behind them.

Q: You did get a feeling for the Japanese mind then to some degree.

Layton: He wasn't a professional teacher but tried to teach me about the Japanese themselves. He said that there's no use of learning a language if you don't know the people and can understand their viewpoint. For my "living in the country," I chose the seaport of Beppu, Kyushu, a hot spring resort, called "the Carlsbad of Japan" -- very famous among Japanese. Many Japanese came there for a holiday. I also chose Beppu because the Japanese Fleet would come in there from time to time for leave and liberty in between exercises at sea. Both the Second Fleet (Cruiser Fleet) and the First Fleet (Battleship Fleet) used Beppu as a recreation port.

Q: Well, it's interesting because I'm sure that gave you some of the, I would guess -- and I'm going to ask you -- do you think that helped you interpret things which you heard of all the various radio traffic and all the various things which you had to put together to make an intelligence evaluation, was this helpful in making it easier for you to interpret?

Layton: These things -- you couldn't say "a" plus "b" plus

"c" equals "d". You couldn't write an equation that would take many unknowns, a, b, c, . . . p, q, r, . . . etc . . ., summarize them and equate them to "z". But each little part had a certain kind of identification or recognition, and if put together properly, could make sense. Sometimes they were right, and sometimes they were wrong, but by and large they worked more satisfactorily with more experience.

Q: But with my understanding of the nuances of the Japanese characters and language is that if you don't put the feeling with the words, it doesn't mean very much.

Layton: No.

Q: I would say that is a very interesting . . .

Layton: There is more nuance than there is directness. Japanese is a very evasive, opaque -- if you want to, you could be very opaque, very non-specific. On the other hand, Japanese can be very specific if such is desired.

Q: Was Japan extremely security-conscious or spy-conscious in the time you were there?

Layton: Up to and through World War II, security-consciousness and spy-consciousness was a mania in Japan. For example, they had large geographical zones called "fortified zones", where even Japanese were frequently arrested for just carrying a camera -- photography, sketching, painting or even carrying a camera was forbidden.

For example, the Peary monument at Uraga (near Yokosuka) was in that fortified zone; right alongside the monument was a sign, very badly done (in what we call "Jap-lish" -- Japanese English) saying "photography no because here". They always had a gendarme there to arrest you if you even had a camera, let alone take a picture of Peary's monument.

If you ask them why, they said, "Oh, you're sure you take a picture with the water behind it for the purpose of amphibious landing intelligence."

Q: I'd like to have you tell me what was the occasion for the four months you spent as assistant naval attache at the American legation at Peiping, China.

Layton: As I was finishing my course of instruction in Japan, orders came to go back to the states to ONI. Then a cable came saying that on completion of my language studies I would go for temporary duty as Assistant Naval Attache to the American Legation, Peiping, China. I went to Peiping (now spelled Peking) and reported for duty to the Naval Attache, Commander Cleveland McCauley USN and the American Minister, Mr. Nelson T. Johnson, both "old China hands". The American minister, Mr. Johnson, told me why I had been sent there. It seems that in the past several months the Japanese Legation

Guard had twice marched out of the Legation Quarter area (contrary to existing rules and international understandings) into the city of Peiping, under the pretext of conducting "night maneuvers". Fortunately, the Chinese had learned of this and had been able to remove all Chinese that were on the Japanese line of march (including paid provacateurs who were to fire at or throw filth on the Japanese soldiers). The Japanese planned to use this "attack" as an excuse to take over and effect a military occupation of Peiping.

Q: They actually moved them out of the houses entirely?

Layton: They moved them out, everyone - young and old - without exception. There was nothing left in any house but the policemen. They were moved out well in advance of the Japanese march. When the Japanese found that their little scheme hadn't worked, they turned around and marched back again. They were called to task by the senior Legation Guard Commander, whom they were required, by protocol to inform prior to leaving the Legation area. As a result of the Boxer Rebellion, the protocol powers -- Japan, America, Great Britain, Austria-Hungary, Russia, Germany, Italy and France were entitled to maintain a Legation Guard for their Legations in (then) Peking; but none of these Legation Guards would go outside legation quarters as a group, armed, without having first cleared it with the Senior Legation Guard Commander. In 1932/33, the Senior Legation Guard Commander was Colonel Gulick, United States

Layton #1 - 19

Marine Corps, the commanding officer of the United States Legation Guard at that time. When the Japanese Legation guard commander was called by Colonel Gulick to protest the violation of protocol, the excuse on this was that they didn't understand English; when the American Legation would protest to the Japanese Legation the Japanese violation of agreements, and the danger of causing an "incident", one of these smiling, be-spectacled, "so-sorry" type of Japanese diplomats would say, "Oh, very sorry, very sorry for you, but we have no one who can speak English to notify Colonel Gulick." The U.S. authorities, knowing that they were being toyed with, requested (through the state department in Washington) that the Navy Department send a Marine graduate of the language course in Tokyo to the legation guard for duty, so that they would have a Japanese linguist available, and the Japs would have no "excuse". My job, now was to go and make a formal call on all Legation Guard Commanders and the Legation Ministers or Charge d'Affair, and to announce that I was in Peiping as Assistant Naval Attache to maintain a liaison with the Japanese Legation Guard, so as to prevent any misunderstandings. So that was my job. I also made official calls on the Chinese, which was a very interesting and enlightening; these official calls involved drinking tea and various "discussions", usually followed later by Chinese dinners and more informal talks. I was finally placed in immediate contact with the head of the Chinese Intelligence for North China. He assigned one of his staff to work with me regarding the problem of the

Japanese legation guard. As a result, I was informed by Chinese Intelligence when Colonel Aihara and his Japanese Legation Guard were planning to go outside the Legation Quarter on unannounced "night manuevers". They did this once while I was there. I received word that they would do so from Chinese Intelligence, and as previously agreed notified the American Legation and Colonel Gulick of the time that Colonel Aihara planned to depart the Gate fronting the "glacis." I went there and greeted Colonel Aihara when he came through the gates. I called out to him, in Japanese in a loud voice (so that his troops and his staff could all hear) "I thought you promised to telephone me before marching your troops outside the Legation Quarter. I will now lose face before Colonel Gulick - who you promised to notify. However, when I was told that you were going to hold "night maneuvers" this morning, and I had not heard from you, I felt certain it was "anti-Japanese propaganda", but came down to greet you, as you see, in case it was the truth, and not "anti-Japanese propaganda". My purpose was to try to embarrass him before his troops and to make him "lose face", if possible.

He and his troops didn't go very far that night. Of course, the Chinese authorities had removed every living soul -- the only things left in the houses along Aihara's line of march were mice or rats. When their march produced no "staged" attack on the Japanese Legation Guard, they returned to the Legation Quarter. This was in late 1932 - mid-late November, I believe. I think that the Japanese came to realize that the Chinese knew when they were going to move out and try to start an "incident," and would be able to forestall them. Sometime later the minister, Mr. Johnson, sent for me and said that he wanted me to go to Manchuria and carry an oral message to the Counsel General in Harbin, one he couldn't send by mail and one he didn't want to telegraph, even in code. In addition, I was to tell all of our Russian language students, navy and Marines, then in Harbin (Manchuria), that they would be withdrawn gradually and to make all their personal plans accordingly but not to discuss it with others. The Japanese had been in Manchuria since they seized it in September '31; after September '31 they would not allow any of the foreign naval or military attaches in Tokyo to go to Manchuria; they would admit that it was Chinese territory but use the excuse that "it was unsafe as they were fighting bandits." When I had finished my Japanese language instruction in September 1932, the Embassy had proposed that I go there for a visit but it was turned down by the Japanese for the above reasons.

Q: Who had proposed that?

Layton: The American naval attache through the American Embassy.

Therefore I was glad to have the opportunity to visit Manchuria. Enroute I decided to make contact with an American (married to a Japanese) who lived in Dairen and worked

Layton #1 - 22

for the Southern Manchuria Railroad, a Japanese government monopoly. I knew that the South Manchuria Railway had custody of the Port Arthur naval base, which the Japanese had "placed in reserve" due to budget shortages during the depression. I thought that if I went to see my friend there, I might get a chance to go see this "civilian dockyard" which was under no published restrictions, being run by the South Manchuria Railroad; that I could inspect it under the pretext that in case an American naval vessel in the area needed to have some repairs, what could be done; to ascertain the nature of repairs that would be made, the drydock size, depth over the sill, and capacities of the machine shops and things like that.

I wanted to see Port Arthur also because of its fame in history of the Russo-Japanese War.

Well, it worked; I had known him previously in Tokyo -- and I had entertained him and his wife there. After calling on him and some social talk I mentioned that I'd like to see Port Arthur, and its battlefields and the old Russian defense works. We spent the morning looking over the battlefields then at lunch, I casually suggested that we might go through the "old machine shops and stuff" that the South Manchuria Railway now ran at Port Arthur, using my pretext of U.S. Naval repair probabilities. He telephoned his Boss, a civilian in the S.M.R., who gave an O.K.- So I not only "inspected" the Navy Yard, they also furnished me accurate, official data on the drydocks, repair facilities and capacities, etc.

Q: But you had to keep all of this in your head.

Layton: Not all of it. He gave me certain data which I wrote down; I assembled the data, addressed a letter in Japanese to myself (using my Chinese characters) in Peiping with a return address of my friend in Dairen and put it in an ordinary post box with less that the correct amount of postage. The reason for "less than the correct amount of postage" was that on delivery, the receiver will have to pay the "postage due" plus a small fine or penalty. That was the safest and best way of having it delivered as a combination of special delivery and registered mail. Since it having money "due", it would be receipted for at each Post Office that handled it.

Then went up to Harbin and carried out my instructions. I tried to go out to Tsitsihar where the Japanese army was getting ready to make a drive across the Hsingan mountains. The Japanese authorities wouldn't let me go, saying that the road was out and the area was "infested with bandits". While I was wandering around Harbin I saw that the Jap army was picking up every piece of transport and rolling stock they could collect; all kinds of trucks, carriages, and horses were being loaded on flat cars in the railway freight-yards. I reported to Peiping (and ONI via Peiping) that the expected Japanese push across the Hsingan to the westward was about to commence. While in Harbin I learned through a friend in the Japanese Consulate General there that there had been "ill feeling" between the Japanese army and the Japanese navy in Manchuria. I didn't know there was a Japanese navy in Manchuria. I didn't know there was a Japanese navy there but my friend said, "Oh yes. Here's some old Japanese newspapers that tell about this."

So I spent a day going through all the old Japanese newspapers concerning the matter: it was about a big Sungari River flood that had taken place that summer, July 1932. The flood cut off all the railroads from Harbin, thus cutting off Harbin from its line of supply to Mukden. It also cut off all the Japanese army detachments that were scattered here and there, occupying North Manchuria. It cut off their food and their ammunition supply. The Japanese Army was surrounded by water and they didn't have any boats. Many were drowned. The Navy came to their rescue with some barges and tugs. The Navy also rescued some of these isolated army groups and moved them to high ground. Moreover, the Navy supplied them with food, drinking water and supplies.

Then the Japanese army realized that their detachments were immobile, so they asked the Navy to set up some naval mobile detachments. So the navy put some boiler plate on river barges and the tugs to push them, and put a field - piece and some machine guns on the barges with naval gunners, and established control of the area by running up and down the flooded areas. The Japanese army was very pleased until the water went down; then they wanted the navy to stop being the North Manchurian Navy, to disarm their barges.

Most of this was in the newspaper, accounts which only hinted at the army-navy rift. So I went to call on the Japanese Resident Naval Officer in Harbin, whom I had met before in Tokyo. I told him that I wanted to talk about this great feat they had done on the Sungari River, and all of its branches, in rescuing the Japanese army in this time of the great flood, particularly "when there were all these bandits around." He gave me a full outline of the navy's rescue of the army's position in Northern Manchuria, and how they said 'thank you very much, now you put us back down there' and how they wanted the navy to be their line of supply now. The navy was to become an army supplemental supply force.

I know that this antipathy, misunderstanding, and disregard for service feelings had gone deep in their army and navy for years. This was rather typical. So in World War II we knew that there would be this antipathy, this lack of cooperation. Some people think the Navy-MacArthur or Army-Navy disagreements in the Pacific were something but they don't know what they were talking about. Ours was just the finest of cooperation, compared to that of the Japanese services.

Q: That's interesting. And then you went back from there to the Legation.

Layton: Yes. Then the day before New Year's Eve 1932 one

of the marines that I knew quite well of the legation guard was . . .

Q: Do you mean 1933?

Layton: 1932 -- New Year's Eve, not New Year's Day. That would be '33.

Q: I see, I see. Excuse me.

Layton: But he told me that he had information from Chinese, which he thought I should know about; that the Japanese army in Manchuria near the Great Wall were ready to make a move of some kind, but they didn't know exactly where. They thought it would be toward the Great Wall, which as you know, is not far from Peiping.

So I got in touch with the Chinese intelligence people and they said they had heard rumors like this, but such rumors arose all the time. They wanted to talk to the Marine officer and did, as a result of which we two received official "passes" to visit the Shanhaikwan area which is on the exact border between Manchuria and North China. Shanhaikwan is the town where the Great Wall meets the sea, where the Great Wall starts -- and where the Peking-Mukden railroad goes through the wall enroute to Mukden.

So we went there and crossed over into a strip of Manchuria which had not been occupied by Japan yet. We went down there and learned from the natives that there were increasing concentrations of troops near there, moving toward Shanhaikwan. We went far enough to see for ourselves that this was true, then we moved back and got the word out that the Japanese army was moving up with the objective of capturing Shanhaikwan. They took it that night. Then we got word from Chinese Intelligence that additionally the Japanese would make a move against, or through the Great Wall, at a pass called Ku' Pei' kou. So we went scurrying up there and after the Japs arrived at Ku' Pei' kou about the 2nd or 3rd of January, I went back to my duties in Peking. I left there in late February when Major Jerry Monahan of the Marine Corps, a former Japanese language student, arrived in Peking and took over the special intelligence assignment I had had. I was glad to go home. I had been away from the U.S. for a long time.

Q: Then you returned from the Far East to ONI for five months. What was that? A major debriefing?

Layton: A debriefing and starting the plotting of strategic industry: strategic power grids, and so forth in Japan; to be used later, as it turned out, as World War II bombing target information.

As I had been away from the Fleet for a long time, I was ordered to the USS <u>Pennsylvania</u>. My first assignment was Turret One and First Division officer. A year later the

Layton #1 - 28

Executive Officer sent for me and said, "I know you like it where you are but we have to have somebody back in the Fourth Division, on the quarterdeck; that division is not up to standard, and we're sending you back there." I straightened out the difficulties in the division and changed their procedure of turret loading and firing; we won the Navy E that year in the 14-inch, 45 caliber turret competition, which won me the Secretary of the Navy's Commendation letter for the highest turret performance in that category. That was the first E turret the Pennsylvania had had in many years and it was a source of pride to everybody concerned. After the first year, Admiral Reeves came on board the flagship with his staff; on his staff was my old friend Joe Rochefort, whose title was Assistant Operations Officer, but he was also the Intelligence Officer for the Commander-in-Chief, U.S. Fleet.

From time to time, Japanese naval tankers would come in San Pedro to fill with fuel -- this was part of their espionage operations, radio monitoring and interception while enroute to and from across the Pacific, and to contact local citizens in Long Beach and San Pedro. There was an active Japanese-Patriotic Society ashore in that area. By Navy custom and regulations, where a foreign man-of-war came in port, it was to be boarded by a representative of the Senior Officer Present and a "boarding call" made. I was made the CinC's boarding officer (suggested of Joe Rochefort) on all Japanese naval ships by Admiral Reeves.

Layton #1 - 29

Q: Well, you spoke Japanese which made it a natural assignment.

Layton: When the Japanese tanker captain would make his official protocol call on the flagship, he would be received by the chief of staff or the senior operations officer; Joe Rochefort would then sit in as a staff representative to ask pertinent questions, if he had any at that time. This official call had to be returned officially by a member of the staff -- calls had to be made and returned -- so when this call was returned, Joe Rochefort would usually make the return call. In the fall of 1934 (I believe it was), Joe sent for me and said, "There's a man ashore here who works with the 11th Naval District. He's a doctor who works with ONI's undercover organization ashore that keeps track of what's going on in the Japanese community. He's just discovered, through his contacts, that the Japanese naval tanker which came in today (it was the Tsurumi or the Sata as I recall) has some special Japanese film which they intend to show to the Japanese association ashore tomorrow night. We believe that this film is subversive and we'd like to have you help the undercover boys ashore on this matter. I had not made the boarding call on this ship as I had the OOD watch at the time and Rochefort had made it. I went ashore with Rochefort, was introduced to the "Doctor" and asked what I was to do. He said, "Well, I haven't got any instructions for you other than, if I were you, I wouldn't look too prosperous. I would not shave tomorrow and I'd wear some old clothes. I don't know how to get you into their meeting to see their film, so we'll just have to find a way to get you into this meeting to see what's going on." I went ashore the next day, met the Doctor who was accompanied by a professional naval intelligence agent. They drove me over to see the manager of the Shell Oil installation on Signal Hill, whose auditorium had been rented by the Japanese Citizens Patriotic Society of Orange County for the meeting. The Doctor explained to the Manager that naval intelligence wanted me to be present at the meeting. The manager said that since the Japanese had rented the hall, they had the right to deny any non-member admittance and that gaining entrance would be a problem.

We talked it over for a while and the naval intelligence agent said, "Well, I have a suggestion. They've got a motion picture projector and the Shell Oil Company has fire insurance on their building here. Why can't Layton, pose as the Insurance Company's representative and be present to be sure that everything is done in accordance with the law, and the insurance policy for the prevention of fire during a motion picture showing, particularly so, since there is no projection-booth. He could enforce a no smoking provision during the showing of this film. We can arrange to get a fire extinguisher for Layton and we'll be outside in case of any trouble.

So that evening I went to the Clubhouse. I had provided myself with some false credentials like "New England Mutual Life Insurance Company," (or some such) stating in effect that I was to be present, to be sure that the fire insurance conditions were not violated and the insurance voided during public meetings on the Shell Oil Company properties.

When the Japanese chairman of this local Patriotic Association arrived there with their group, including the sailors from the tanker, I explained to them in English my "job" and showed my (false) credentials. I pretended not to know any Japanese. They had some discussion in Japanese about me being present which I could understand. Then they told me in English my presence wasn't necessary. I brought out the paper and I said: "Me no here, no movies." By that time some two or three hundred Japanese had arrived in the Hall and were taking seats. As the program was to show these motion pictures, they had to put up with my being there. I went around and put out cigarettes here and there. Whenever a Japanese didn't understand me, I'd point to his cigarette, take it out of his hand, and step on it, saying, "No smoke. No smoke." I had put a large fire extinguisher (the kind you turn upside down to use) adjacent to the motion projector which had been bought from the Japanese naval tanker. A curious Japanese sailor from the tanker in examining it turned it upside down and gets a face full of foam and, of course, there was foam all over the floor. So I had to work hard then and afterward to clean up this foam. It removed the wax finish from the floor; it was an awful mess.

Because I had to clean up this mess and made a commotion about it, the chairman of the Japanese Association came over after the show was over and gave me five dollars "for my trouble."

When the meeting had ended the doctor, and the professional ONI agent joined me in a bar in Long Beach where we drank up most of that five dollars, celebrating the success of our operation.

Q: Well, was it subversive?

Layton: Yes. Designed to arouse Japanese patriotism, it showed the "brave Japanese" assaulting Chinese positions, of Chinese retreating, and the usual scene of soldiers standind on top of a wall shouting "Banzai" with the Japanese flag flying. One film was to show contempt for Democracies: it showed the President of the United States, Mr. Roosevelt, (acted by Yul Brenner, the comedian) who would put on comic hats and do "take-offs" on President Roosevelt's mannerisms. Other actors would mock other elected leaders of Democracies, with film clips of strike breaking or rioting, intersperced. Then they would show the Emperor, with everybody bowing showing the pomp and ceremony. It was pretty "corny" but this was their way of telling them that their Emperor system was best, that Democracy as represented by the American President was no good. Another scene was typical: an animated cartoon showed J.P. Morgan pushing a wheelbarrow full of money, over bodies of the poor, the downcast, quite unpleasant.

I wrote a report for Joe, which was then written up for

Admiral Reeves and went back to ONI, with a copy for the local Naval District Commandants.

The following year I was still in the <u>Pennsylvania</u>, now as Senior Watch Officer. The ship was enroute to San Francisco as part of a fleet maneuver when word came that Joe wanted to see me on an important matter.

I went to the Fleet Staff area; Joe closed the door and said that certain instructions which he had received were now official: I would be detached as soon as the ship docked at Hunters' Point and would proceed to the Bremerton Navy yard, where I'd go aboard the <u>Brazos</u>, which was sailing to Dutch Harbor. He said that a Japanese spy was around Dutch Harbor and the Commander-in-Chief wants that spy put away, so he won't be able to observe and report on our ships. The <u>Brazos</u> is scheduled to get there just before the Scouting Force arrives at Dutch Harbor. He said, "You'll have to catch this evening's train for Seattle to be able to catch the <u>Brazos</u> before she sails from Bremerton, and you must sail in the <u>Brazos</u> for Dutch Harbor." He then gave me my temporary additional duty orders signed by Admiral Reeves. Joe had reminded me that there was also an officer on the staff (Lt. Comdr. Wilbur Lockhart, an aerologist who had been stationed up in Dutch Harbor) who might have some contacts there; that I should see him and check out whether he could give me any letters of introduction to local authorities in Dutch Harbor. I went to him and told him I had some very important business up there for the Commander-in-Chief and asked his assistance.

Layton #1 - 34

He gave me a run down on the general situation in the Dutch Harbor area -- he knew two people up there -- one area, and letters of introduction to the Postmaster (who was also the Federal Judge for that area) and to the local manager of the Alaska Commercial Company. He told me that the site of the civilian community was Illilliuk, which was also the location of the Post office and the A.C. Company, while Dutch Harbor, the naval base, was located on a small island in the bay. I caught the evening train to Seattle, crossed over to Bremerton and reported aboard the Brazos for transportation to Dutch Harbor. Enroute I told the captain of the Brazos that I would want to go ashore at Illilliuk as soon as we anchored in Unalaska Bay. He promised to send me ashore in the first boat, along with the mail orderly.

Upon anchoring off Dutch Harbor, early in the morning, I went ashore in civilian clothes to see what I could do. I asked that the boat, and the mail orderly, wait at the dock for a while, in case I had any urgent messages for the ship to send to the Commander-in-chief relating to my mission. I went to the Postmaster, told him I had a letter of introduction, which I handed to him, and asked to talk with him in private, as what I had to say was highly confidential business of the United States. He closed the post office window and invited me into an adjacent office. There I told him that I was on orders from the Commander-in-Chief to come up there and see to it that a Japanese spy was put out of circulation, and that I needed his help. He said, "Ah, we've only got one Japanese here; he is Mr. Shimizu from Seattle. But he's not a spy, is he?"

I told him that I presumed that since he was the only Japanese there, he must be the man that I was instructed to have placed "out of circulation", and again asked what he could do to help me. He said, "Well, I think the man to help you is my friend, George. He's the Federal Marshall for this territory, a graduate of the University of Washington, half Aleut and married to an Aleut, and a good man . . . . " He told me to tell George that he had sent me, adding that George was a man I could trust and that if there was anything that could be done to help, he, (as the Federal Marshall) could probably do it.

So I asked directions, and walked up the unpaved road of the village to the marshall's home, which was also his office and the Federal Jail. After telling him of my mission and my need for his advice and help, he said that he would be happy to help me in any way he could. After thinking over the matter for a short time he said: "From what I hear this Jap, Shimizu, has been in violation of the law here for some time by bootlegging; but I have to have a complaint and evidence." "Why don't you go down and buy a bottle of booze from him, bring it back to me and file a complaint, and I'll take him into custody. Then we'll take him down to the Federal Judge (and Postmaster) who can then handle the matter as the law provides." I agreed. He described the place where Shimizu usually was, back of the only street in town. I went down there and knocked on the door and when a Japanese opened it I said, "I understand you've got some booze here for me and I need it very badly. I just got in on the boat."

He looked at me and said, "That'll be $2.00." He handed me over the bottle and I gave him the money and walked out and down to the corner where the marshall was waiting for me. I said, "Here's the booze," and he said, "You better taste it to be sure that it's alcoholic." I took a taste; it was alcoholic all right -- like shellac! He then marched up and arrested Shimizu for violation of federal laws: possession of untaxed alcoholic liquor and selling same without a license.

We took him down to the post office building where the postmaster ushered us to another room having a sign on it "Federal District Court," and announced: "Court's open."

The marshall said, "The charge is selling booze in violation of federal statutes" -- naming them.

When asked, "How do you plead?", Shimizu replied, "Yes, I sold him booze." The Judge replied: "30 days,", so Shimizu went to jail; I thanked the Marshall for his quick action on behalf of the Commander-in-Chief, and the United States as a whole, and for safeguarding the national interest. He said that there was still another angle of the problem; that Shimizu had a gal downtown, the town whore, who also might be his assistant, to help him report what the Fleet was doing, how many ships etc; that she may be planted to gather information from the sailors, so perhaps she should be put in jail, too. I asked what could be done and he said that he could put her in jail if he had proof of her prostitution. I told him that the mail-orderly was down at the dock waiting for me. I went down to the mail orderly and I told him that the Federal Marshall believed this town whore might be a part of a Jap spy ring; that if he'd go to her, and pay her $2.00 (which I would give him) and come and testify concerning her prostitution, the marshall would throw her in jail. He agreed. As a result, she also drew a jail sentence. In those days Alaska was under federal law; the jail was, as I said, part of the Federal Marshall's house; his wife acted as female jailor. That evening, the whore asked her to pass a note to Shimizu, the Jap, not knowing that she was the Marshall's wife. She agreed, but gave the note to the marshall, who sent word to me. I recommended that the note be copied, and the original passed on. She told him of her arrest. They passed notes to each other thereafter. Finally, Shimizu asked for letterpaper and an envelope "to write a letter to his parents." It was in Japanese, the envelope addressed to the Tokai Trading company in Seattle. The Marshall sent word to me and showed me the letter, which was on his desk. I asked if it had been placed in a "U.S. Mail" box and he said no, not yet. I asked him to be a witness that I was not violating the postal regulations by opening that letter.

I opened the letter and read his report (in Japanese) that he had been arrested and that he was sorry but he wouldn't be able to do what was expected of him and furthermore, his friend, who had helped him by "contacts" was in

Layton #1 - 38

jail, too. He was awfully sorry to report this.

In the meantime I had sent a message through the <u>Brazos</u> to the Fleet flagship "for Joe - mission accomplished." I learned later on that Shimizu and the whore, when released were declared undesirable, and deported from Alaska.

Q: Was that Fleet Problem 16?

Layton: I suppose it was. I've forgotten the number.

Q: I know you had a Letter of Commendation as well for your special performance of Fleet Problem 16. It sounds as though it might be.

Layton: That may have been it. I had forgotten about the Letter of Commendation.

Then I got my orders to go aboard the USS <u>Tarbell</u>, which although a part of the Scouting Force, was ordered to remain at Dutch Harbor, awaiting instructions. The State Department wanted a mission performed up there. In years past the Japanese Ministry of Fisheries sent out so-called "research" ships to the Aleutians, to study "ecology and sea life, and such things." Actually these ships came to the Aleutians to spy on beaches, fortifications, weather, tides, currents, etc. Instructions soon came saying that in response to a Japanese request for their "research-fisheries ship", HAKUYO Maru, to visit the Aleutians in mid-May, the U.S. Department of State

had approved provided the same procedures, adopted by the
Japanese in the case of U.S. destroyers visits to the Kurile
Islands in connection with the U.S. Army aviators' 'round
the world flight in 1923, were adhered to. The procedures
were -- the minute the U.S. destroyer entered Japanese waters,
a Japanese destroyer came alongside and put a Japanese naval
officer on board the U.S. destroyer as an observer, remaining
aboard as long as it was within Japanese territorial waters;
when the U.S. destroyer left, the Japanese destroyer also
got underway and when the U.S. ship reached the edge of
Japanese territorial waters, the Japanese naval officer would
leave this U.S. destroyer and go back to his regular ship.
This procedure would be repeated if a U.S. destroyer again
entered another island's territorial waters. The Tarbell
was to stand by, and when the HAKUYO Maru, or other Japanese
fisheries or other ships entered territorial waters of the
United States in the Aleutian Islands, I was to go aboard
that Japanese ship, explain my mission and stay aboard as
"liaison officer" as long as it remained in U.S. territorial
waters. When it left, I would return to the USS Tarbell,
which would be standing by; the Tarbell would then trail,
at a proper distance, the Japanese vessel, ready to put me
aboard again if it entered U.S. waters. Well, the captain
of the Tarbell wasn't too happy about this but, it was, at
least, something different -- mostly standing by waiting for
word that the HAKUYO Maru, or other fishing "research" vessels
were going to arrive. A Navy photographic squadron under

Layton #1 - 40

Lieutenant "Cat" Brown (later Admiral "Cat" Brown) was conducting the annual Aleutian photographic survey; of course, there was bad weather up there, so they could fly very little but they did some scouting for us to see if they could see any Japanese ships approaching the Aleutian islands. Well, we waited and we waited; we had no notification of their intended arrival dates. On Memorial Day the Tarbell received a radio dispatch ordering it back to San Diego; the Japanese "research ship's" visit to the Aleutians had been cancelled -- probably because of the arrangements for a U.S. "liaison officer" to be aboard would prevent their objective of intelligence collection.

Q: So that was your Fleet Problem 16, I guess. Let's see now, do you have any more incidents aboard the Pennsylvania? That was a three year tour, from '33 to '36.

Layton: Oh, there was one more. It was earlier in my tour when the Pennsylvania went to the Bremerton Navy Yard. The Commandant of the Navy Yard sent for me and said, "I understand you're a Japanese linguist." I told him I held an official accreditation of interpreter and translater in that language." He said that the Treasury representative from Seattle wants to talk to you. The U.S. Treasury Department man said that they had some material which they wanted me to examine. He said he was with the Narcotics Division. So I then got orders to go over to their offices in Seattle and listened to some recordings. I translated and transcribed those parts that were audible; some of the recording was so bad that there was little but hissing and scratching in places. When I had finished they thanked me very much.

Q: Was that anything of particular interest?

Layton: The Treasury agent sent me a clipping about four or five months later which reported a large seizure of narcotics, which had been smuggled in through Portland. He wrote on it: "You'll note this with interest."

I suppose that whatever it was I had translated for him (which didn't make any sense to me at that time) was some fact or event which they could use, which helped make the reported seizure.

Q: You must have gotten a sense of contribution again.

Layton: Yes, I was glad to be of assistance; it wasn't something I had thought of when I first took the Japanese language.

Q: No. And so now our next item of interest will be your assignment to ONI in June of 1936.

Layton: Yes. After three years on the Pennsylvania, I was detached with orders to report to ONI. In the meantime, by personal letters to ONI and in Personnel Assignment cards, I had indicated that I wanted to be assigned as assistant

Layton #1 - 42

naval attache in Tokyo, so I could continue to use my Japanese in a practical way. By personal letter, ONI said that they had already committed this job to someone else. When I reported in to ONI, they told me not to give up hope of going to Tokyo, as they might change their minds some time in the future. In the meantime, they were going to assign me to Op-20G -- that's the Communications Intelligence section of the Department of Naval Communications. They told me that one of my principal duties there would be to bring any information or intelligence that resulted from my work there to the attention of the Director of Naval Communications, the Director of Naval Intelligence and his deputy, and should they so instruct me, to the Chief of Naval Operations and the Head of the War Plans Section of CNO.

Q: Who were the people?

Layton: Captain Pulleston was the Director of Naval Intelligence. Captain Stapler was the Deputy Director of Naval Intelligence and I believe Captain Courtney -- I'm not real sure -- maybe it was <u>Admiral</u> Courtney, who was the Director of Naval Communications.

Q: So you were working for two bosses at that time.

Layton: Yes, in a sense. When I went to Op-20G, I was assigned to the Z section which is the translation section of communications intelligence. The head of Op-20 (Naval Communications) was, as I said, Captain Courtney. The head of Op-20G (Communications Intelligence) was Lieutenant Commander Safford. He wasn't an active director; he was sort of a research-minded recluse, off in a cubbyhole by himself. The actual executive who ran Op-20G was Lieutenant Wenger. It was there I first made my acquaintance with many of the fine characters in Op-20G. At that time, my immediate task, in addition to translating anything that might be available currently, was to conduct recovery and research on the Japanese Navy's "blue code." This was one of the most interesting and fascinating facets of the use of the Japanese language.

This was not their current code; the blue code was not being used; ONI and Op-20G wanted to continue to recover its values so as to extract all the information that was available in the thousands of coded intercepts on file, but whose text was incomplete for lack of code values. As an example, one of the messages that I took up for research and code-recovery (because it was short) dealt with the "Haruna", which had been (by Japanese announcement) converted to a training ship, and had later on undergone a modernization. She was listed in "Janes" (and officially by Japan) as a "training ship" with a speed of less than 20-knots, something like 18.5 knots. When I had completed code recovery research, and translated the short message it said that the "Haruna" had just finished making 32.05 knots on her official speed trials on completion of overhaul and modernization. There was no error in this; I checked and rechecked the numerical values against many usages such as dates and times in other messages to clearly establish their accuracy.

Such valuable little tidbits like this would appear from time to time during my research; I would take each of these up to the Director of Naval Intelligence and his deputy; sometimes they'd go to the Chief of Naval Operations and always the Chief of Naval Communications. The Head of the Far East Section of ONI would keep these cards in a special sealed envelope in a safe until they could be used; such sensitive items could only be used when the source of the intelligence could be concealed. So that before World War II, Naval Intelligence publications carried the Haruna as having the "official" maximum speed of about 20 knots, but were "updated" just before the war, to reflect more authentic data. Officers who had studied their intelligence publications were not surprised when the "Haruna" made high speed run ins to bombard Guadalcanal. During this research I found that some code values just didn't "fit"; the more one worked, the more confused you got and therefore, something in the code recovery was wrong.

After analyzing it for several weeks, I told Captain Wenger that in a certain section, covering the Japanese mandated Islands, the code groups for geographical locations were in error and should be re-done. He approved.

After about two months work the new recoveries were

Layton #1 - '45

entered and checked; things looked better; now messages relating to their mandated Islands began to make sense.

This started my great interest in the Mandates; I had to study every one of those islands, all about them. Working on them, I found the Japanese navy had been using Ulithi as a secret fleet anchorage during their 1933 fleet problem.

Kossol Passage, for example, was also used as a secret anchorage for an Advance Force in that fleet problem; they also build "emergency landing fields" which planes from their carriers used on the island of Pagan and also on Minami Iwo Jima, (that's Iwo Jima). By these messages, we knew they used various islands in the mandates for special purposes during their maneuvers; this gave valuable clues, indicating what would be their intended use of them for wartime. (It is interesting to note that we made use of this information during the War in the Pacific. From my work, I was satisfied that they were not fortified at <u>that</u> time, which brings up something of later interest. I had a very fine introduction to the Japanese mandated Islands, which proved to be most valuable later on when I served on the CinC U.S. Fleet staff with Admirals Richardson and Kimmel, just before World War II.

Soon after I joined Admiral Richardson's staff in December 1940, I went over to see Rochefort in January 1941.* He was then head of the Communications Intelligence Unit at Pearl Harbor. He told me that the Japanese navy had just changed their call-signs, including their "WE" address system. He

---

*According to Captain Rochefort's official biography, he did not report to Pearl Harbor as officer in charge of the Combat Intelligence Unit, Pacific Ocean Areas, until June

Layton #1 - 46

said, "Here's a good chance for you to help us. We're too busy to work on the "WE" address cipher as we're working on call sign recovery, so you can work on the "WE" address system — it's a simple-substitution cipher. So I went to work and pretty soon up came repetitions of "SA.I.PA.N" and "PA.A.RA.U" (Saipan and Palau) in "spelled-out" addresses. When someone didn't have a call sign book, they spelled out the addressee of a message by using a simple substitution cipher. The "PA" of SAIPAN and the "PA" of PALAO were identical; later the same "PA" came up for the "PA" of PAGAN. After quite a while, examining hundreds of intercept messages other "values" are recovered, and like a cryptogram in the newspapers or magazines, the substitution cipher of the "WE" address system is recovered. By late January 1941 it became apparent that the Japanese were up to something unusual in the mandated Islands. Many civilian ships were going there under either a naval charter or as newly requisitioned supply ships of the navy. The amount of traffic addressed in the "WE" address cipher was vastly increased over anything ever experienced. The "WE" address system solution gave addresses such as "Officer in charge of Coast Defense Guns at Saipan," "Wotje," "Jaluit," etc - "Senior Officer at Naval airfield at ROI" (Ruotto" - on Kwajalein), on "Saipan", "Tinian", "Truk", "Wotje", and "Woleai" - "For Submarine base at Kwajalein," and messages regarding ammunition storage, radio stations, barracks, and Defense Detachments at many places in the

Mandated Islands. This build up was reported to Admiral Richardson, and when he turned his command over to Admiral Kimmel, I briefed the latter in the presence of the former concerning this militarization of the Mandated Islands in violation of Japan's solemn promises. The intercepts from which the vast majority of this intelligence was derived were made at Guam. Guam intercept station forwarded the originals to CNO (Op-20G) and a copy of them to Rochefort's unit. No copies were sent to CinC Pacific Fleet. These were raw intercepts and contained much enciphered traffic. Rochefort used those intercepts as technical back up for analysis of his unit's intercepts. I extracted the intelligence that I could obtain from decrypting the "WE" addresses for my boss, the Commander-in-Chief of the Fleet, as permitted by the very stringent instructions (secret) concerning the handling of intercept traffic. (Radio Intelligence Publication #3). Admiral Richardson was visibly impressed with the data I presented him and specifically mentioned "ominous developments in the Japanese Mandates" to Admiral Kimmel when he visited the flagship, at sea, right after Admiral Richardson learned that Admiral Kimmel would succeed him.

After Admiral Kimmel assumed command, he wanted to be briefed once more on the Japanese militarization of the Mandates and I reviewed each island with him, where they were, and what was being done on each of them; the organization of their fleet and its past activities and capabilities. I found my experience in Op-20G in straightening out the code recovery for the mandated islands and my research in their maneuvers there was a great assistance in briefing the new CinC.

When Admiral Kimmel was to go back to Washington for a conference with Admiral Stark in June of 1941, I said, "When you're back there, I think it would be well to ask how they view this Jap activity in the Mandates." Our view was that they would't start this militarization of the Mandated Islands unless they had some need, militarily, for such bases. Admiral Kimmel made a note to ask CNO about that. He hadn't been back there a day when in came a nasty top-secret dispatch from Chief of Naval Operations to Commander-in-Chief, U.S. Fleet which said in effect: it has come to the attention of the Chief of Naval Operations that the Fleet Intelligence Officer of the Pacific Fleet has in his possession certain vital information dealing with the militarization of Mandated Islands by Japan, which he has not seen fit to report to the Chief of Naval Operations or to ONI. You will immediately send this information to this office in this same cipher system, etc., etc. I have never seen a more demanding, a more emphatic, or a more nasty dispatch.

Q: It's hard to believe.

Layton: It's hard to believe.

Q: Because they had all the information and had it all along.

Layton #1 - 49

Layton: That's just it. Op-20G had it in their files but they hadn't done anything about it. I have never heard the full details of this, but I assume they had some Yeoman or clerk file them away without a critical examination. Hence ONI, and CNO, knew nothing of this matter, which we assumed Op-20G had passed on to them.

Q: They had it and didn't pass it on to the people who needed to know.

Layton: I don't think they ever read those intercepts.

Q: You don't think Safford ever read it.

Layton: I don't think anyone back there examined those Guam intercepts. That's the only explanation that I can conceive of. Had anyone examined them, the new "WE" address code, and the wealth of intelligence data in the decryption of the addressees would have impelled the examiner to bring it to someone's attention in Op-20G and thence to ONI and CNO.

The answer from Pearl Harbor to CNO's blast set forth all of the information available; it consisted of three closely typewritten dispatch blanks. The last paragraph said, in effect; All of this information came from intercept of station George (Guam) which was addressed to the Chief of Naval Operations (Op-20G) with a copy to Station HYPO (Rocheforts Unit) but not in any way addressed to Commander-in-Chief, United States Fleet. In accordance with RIP-3

(Radio Intelligence Publication 3), the Fleet Intelligence Officer was allowed to examine this material for tactical information of value of the Fleet. It seems inconceivable to "this command" (CinC Pacific Fleet) that the Chief of Naval Operations was unaware of intelligence addressed to that office and which was obtained by the Intelligence Officer Pacific Fleet through liaison.

When Admiral Kimmel returned from Washington, I asked him what had happened to bring that "blast" from CNO. He replied that when he asked them about the mandate-militarization they were shocked as they knew absolutely nothing of the matter. He said that when they had investigated, they found that "Some commander had it on file but had never looked at it" -- that he was busy on some other matter.

Q: But what I don't understand is why CNO in writing that message -- I shouldn't say why but where they got their information that you had this information.

Layton: Kimmel went back there and took up the subject of the Japanese militarization of the mandates with Stark, as I'd asked him to. Stark said he never heard of it. So then Stark sent for his Director of Naval Intelligence, but he had never heard of it, either. So, they sent back this message saying, in effect, we don't know anything about a Japanese military buildup in the mandates. Kimmel says he gets such intelligence from his intelligence officer, Layton,

Layton #1 - 51

who must have received something from somewhere, and didn't let us know.

Q: So they're trying to get off the hook by saying that you have it.

Layton: No, they're mad; properly mad because they don't have information that the Chief of Naval Operations should have, since the CinCPacific Fleet has it. They wanted to know "what are you doing holding back this intelligence?"

Q: I see. They did have it.

Layton: They didn't know they had it.

Q: I know that but they had it and in order to get off the hook and get off the pan themselves they say that you had it and didn't let them know.

Layton: This is right.

Q: When in fact they had it in their own office but the man who was supposed to have it and bring it to the attention of the right person hadn't done it.

Layton: The raw information was in their files somewhere but no one had even read it, apparently.

Layton #1 - 52

Q: You don't even think that Safford had read it.

Layton: No.

Q: It's inconceivable to me that messages come in and not be read.

Layton: These weren't messages or dispatches. They were copies of the intercepts, which had been transmitted in Japanese kata kana code, the Japanese equivalent of Morse code. I believe that the intercepts were all in cipher, and hence nothing but a meaningless jumble of romanized Kana symbols. The raw intercept traffic is not readable at a glance since the purpose of the encipherment is to conceal its contents.

Referring again to CNO's nasty dispatch to Pearl Harbor in June 1941 about the intelligence on the Mandates. I wanted to use this dispatch during Congressional Investigation of Pearl Harbor in late 1945, early 1946 but I was told that I couldn't bring anything in that went as far back as July 1941, the cut-off date.

Q: Who told you this?

Layton: The Judge Advocate General of the Navy, who acted for the Secretary of the Navy in matters dealing with the Joint Congressional Investigation of Pearl Harbor. So that

Layton #1 - 53

matter was not brought out at the Pearl Harbor investigation. During this congressional inquiry into Pearl Harbor they were saying "Washington had this, and Washington did this," and even though Pearl Harbor wasn't given the intelligence that Washington had, "Admiral Kimmel should have known this, and should have known that," etc. The CNO dispatch and CinC Pacific reply would have shown a good example of CNO having "dropped the ball" in early 1941, as far as intelligence on Japan was concerned. Since CNO failed to keep Admiral Kimmel informed on intelligence of Japan later in 1941, before Pearl Harbor, the disaster there was largely due to failure in Washington to evaluate properly the intelligence available.

Q: Have you ever been able to make it public at all?

Layton: No. That dispatch CNO sent out, and the reply are still top secret. They have not been declassified. I think the decision not to declassify such things is a part of a cover-up. Let me add something else. In 1941 there was a publication, the "ONI Manual", or some such title, called "ONI 11," that remained in effect throughout the war. It was a registered, classified publication. The registered Publication office in Washington sends out "changes" and "corrections" with notifications to holders to make certain changes, and put in new pages in registered publications. The registered publications officer on Admiral Nimitz's staff at the time (late 1944, I think) Lieutenant Bidwell came around one day saying he had some changes for the ONI manual (which was in my safe). He took custody of it and returned it after making the changes and I put it back in the safe without examining it, as I was busy at that time. I happened to open it some time later and found that the entire section having to do with "duties and responsibilities" of the Chief of Naval Operations (ONI) and CinCof Fleets (Fleet Intelligence Officers) had been removed and no new pages furnished. So, all there was that was written there as of 1940, 1941, and '42, etc., were no longer in the manual. I asked Lt. Bidwell about the replacement pages and he stated none came. I sent Lieutenant Bidwell out among ships in port to see if, by chance, some ship had not yet entered their "changes", so I could get the old pages before they were burned (as ours had been). But there weren't any copies. If any ship hadn't made their changes, they wouldn't admit it. We searched high and low, trying to find one copy, but couldn't; apparently they were all destroyed.

Later, during the Congressional investigation of Pearl Harbor when I wanted to refer to ONI instructions, dealing with the intelligence responsibilities of the Director of Naval Intelligence (Chief of Naval Operations) and their relationship to the responsibilities of the Fleet Intelligence Officer (CinC Pacific Fleet), I could not, because these instructions had become blank pages.

Q: One would know that back in ONI there were the original ones.

Layton #1 - 55

Layton: They wouldn't be produceable.

Q: No, but they would be there, of course.

Layton: Not if they wanted to get rid of them. After all, the Office of Registered Publications of CNO had ordered them removed and destroyed.

Q: You did leave ONI in 1937. Actually your tour of duty there was only about seven months, wasn't it?

Layton: Yes.

Q: And because the vacancy did occur, you were assigned to go to Japan as the assistant naval attache in the American Embassy and I'd like to hear any events that occurred during that period.

Layton: Enroute to Japan in the same ship was the former Russian Naval attache in Washington (whom I had met there) returning to Russia via the Pacific. We became friendly during the voyage and on arrival at Kobe, the Japanese authorities refused to recognize his diplomatic passport and were insisting on searching his belongings when he disembarked. I spoke to the Japanese officials, vouching for his diplomatic status, and when they still remained adamant, I telephoned the Russian Consulate in Kobe, explained the problem. The Russian consul came to the dock and straightened everything out. The Russian Naval and Military attaches in Tokyo thanked me. Four months later when the Japs attacked the Marco Polo Bridge and started the war with China, Captain Kovaleff, the Russian naval attache in Tokyo, came to my office (not into my boss's office, Captain Bemis) with some maps and some written material. Captain Kovaleff said, "Now that they have started fighting, I want to tell you I'm coming to help you." Can I help you?"

I said, "Of course." Then he spread out his map and he showed me the old Chinese "silk route", the famous old trail over the Gobi, over which they were bringing supplies into China.

Q: Marco Polo, wasn't it?

Layton: Yes, the old silk route. He said, "I will tell you how much we are sending now, by what ways, and so forth. I will continue to keep you advised if you wish, without obligation on your part. I want to show you that I am honest with you. If you have any information that will be of interest to me, as would effect our position here, I would appreciate it."

I said, "Captain Kovaleff, I will do all I can. I can only do a limited job and whatever I do, I'll have to clear with our naval attache. Would you come over with me and meet him?"

He said, "Oh, I know him. I'll pay my respects." He seemed to have no desire to deal directly with Captain Bemis. (Captain Bemis was kind of a frosty fellow at times). I told Captain Bemis that Captain Kovaleff had said that, from time to time, he would bring me information having to do with their supplies going into China, and with the particular aircraft which they were furnishing the Chinese, and to keep us advised of what's being done in view of this situation. I suggested that if he thought it proper, I should act as a representative of the naval attache to receive them. Captain Bemis agreed. For some time thereafter, they brought me up to date information which we furnished the Ambassador, and the Counselor of the Embassy; sometimes it was incorporated in Embassy dispatches back to Washington.

Before the China war broke out, we received a dispatch from the Chief of Naval Operations saying that Amelia Earhart was lost in the Pacific somewhere and told the Naval Attache to approach the Japanese, and ask the assistance of any ships they might have down in the Mandated area, on a priority basis. This request (in English) and a formal Japanese translation of it were immediately prepared. After telephoning the Japanese Navy Department for an appointment, I took them to the Navy Department and presented them to Admiral Yamamoto.

Q: Admiral Yamamoto?

Layton: He was then the Vice Minister of the Navy. Official business between the naval attaches and the Japanese Navy Department was through Admiral Yamamoto, the Vice Minister. Routine matters were conducted through one of the Vice Minister's aides, who acted as liaison officer. Thus, he represented the Japanese Navy Ministry while the Naval Attache represented his own Chief of Naval Operations.

Q: Tell me about Yamamoto and then we'll go back to your call about Amelia Earhart.

Layton: As I have always told other people, I have always viewed Yamamoto as a very human, a very real, and a very sincere man. Many Japanese are hard to "get to". They are quite reser sometimes very aloof. One sometimes has the impression that they are like actors in a "Noh drama, wearing false faces or masks to suit their role. With Yamamoto, I got to feel that on social occasions he did not wear his false face. He was my host one time at a theatre party, and another time at a duck hunt (when we played bridge also) and another time at a geisha party. He could be quite relaxed with people and made it a point to go around and talk to each of his guests. He was a very good poker player; against skilled poker players, he almost always won, and he almost invariably won at bridge, too. He was a splendid bridge player.

Q: I would be an admirer of his then.

Layton: He was a "Japanese Champion" at the games of "Go" and "shogi", Japanese games something like chess and checkers. He was hard working and devoted to his profession. He had a lot of steel in his eyes; you could see it if something irritated him for his eyes would become hard and cold; usually, they would be more soft (liquid).

Q: The story goes that if he was not permitted to do the Pearl Harbor operation as he had planned that he would resign.

Layton: I would doubt that. There's a lot of stories of all kinds. I don't believe that he wanted war with America. It is my firm conviction that he, having lived in the U.S. and the Western Hemisphere, was one of the peace party. I have heard from pretty good levels that the one reason he was removed from the Navy Ministry and sent out of Tokyo was because of the hostility of the pro-war advocates. He had opposed the Anti-Comintern Pact with Nazi Germany and Mussolini's Facist Italy. The pro-war faction only got this Pact approved after he had been removed from the Navy Ministry (where he had a voice in politics) to the post of Commander-in-Chief of the Fleet (where he had no voice in politics). I think that Admiral Yamamoto felt that the only way Japan could be successful was to knock out the American Fleet at Pearl Harbor. I don't think his heart was really in it. Now, I feel a certain personal relationship in this because I was the one who took the original intelligence to Admiral Nimitz which resulted in Admiral Yamamoto being shot down in the South Pacific. In this regard Admiral Nimitz said, "Do you think we ought to?" And I said, "Yes, I think we should."

Nimitz sent the message to Admiral Halsey saying that Hamamoto himself will arrive at Buin, at so-and-so a time on so-and-so a date, in two Betty-type bombers, escorted by six zeros. They sent back a response acknowledging Nimitz's dispatch and saying they had the capability of intercepting but would hold off on such action, in view of the sensitivity of the information, until assured by you that you want this carried out. I was pretty sure such a reply would come in, so when it did, I took my draft dispatch to Admiral Nimitz, which went something like: "You are authorized and directed to go ahead with this operation provided all personnel concerned with the operation, particularly the pilots, are briefed that the information comes from Australian coast watchers near Rabaul, whose information in the past has been most timely and helpful." Admiral Nimitz read it over carefully and wrote a postscript on the dispatch: "Best of luck and good hunting."

Q: Mr. Potter has this for his list.

Layton: Yes.

Q: Did you have any sense of regret at all when you realized that your message was . . .

Layton: No. While he had been an official friend of mine,

he was now our enemy. War is, in essence, the destruction of your enemy; as the leader and inspiration of the Japanese Navy he was an important enemy, whose destruction could only benefit our side, in my view. He was the only man in the Japanese Navy (that I knew of) that I felt was very superior, an outstanding symbol of their navy and their Pearl Harbor surprise attack. This is one thing that may have prompted Admiral Nimitz to ask, "Are you sure there are none who can take his place, and be better than he?" I said, "Absolutely none. Absolutely none."

Q: Well, I think we had better go back to the time when you took the note over to the Japanese Ministry about the search for Amelia Earhart.

Layton: There was an article in the Naval Institute Proceedings recently where a Japanese author says that they had never been asked to search for Amelia Earhart. This is false, like much of that article's contents. I took the formal request to the Japanese Navy Department (Naval Ministry) and they acknowledged it; later, they reported that the only ship they had in that area was the Kamoi, a seaplane tender, which had searched in her operations area without results and that the Kamoi had completed its "survey operations" and returned to port.

Q: Would there be any information in the Japanese naval records to which we have not had access which might clarify it?

Layton: They say their records have all been burned; their Navy Department was all burned out, by fire bombs. At the end of the war the Japanese ordered all records to be destroyed.

Q: I wanted to ask you if you were aware of the build-up by the Japanese at that time you were assistant Naval attache in Tokyo. Were there more places off-limits and more restrictions on you or the Japanese people than when you had been there previously?

Layton: At that time, I lived near the Imperial Guard barracks. To go to the Embassy I had to walk in front of the gate of those barracks. Normally, the sentry would pace up and down in front of the gate although he had a little sentry box back, off the sidewalk. Whenever Japan felt militaristic, these sentries would stand guard with fixed bayonets, and when a foreigner passed, would run him off the sidewalk, out into the street. Normally, he would give a loud yell and charge at you with his bayonet, forcing you out into the street. I've seen them drive foreign women and children, off the sidewalk and out into the street; it was, I suppose, just to show that they were rough, tough military people.

Q: Did you have a sense of a militaristic build-up, in Japan.

Layton: Yes, there was no doubt about it. In the summer

I lived in a little seaside place called Hayama; I would come in on the train each day, early in the morning, returning to my home in the evening. The train goes through a large railway center of Shinagawa, where the Japanese army would make up their troop trains, and load their supplies and tanks and armored cars etc. You could see these troop trains assembled in the railway yards, railway cars being loaded with supplies and flat cars being loaded with artillery and motor transport. One could observe what types of troops (infantry, engineers, aviation, artillery) were being called up, reservists joining the colors.

Q: Did you do any specific intelligence activities?

Layton: After the war spread to Shanghai, I went there to observe the fighting and contact some of our marines there who had been back of the Chinese lines, to learn all I could of the facts of the situation. I went over carrying the Embassy Pouch to Shanghai, returning I was carrying the pouch from Shanghai to our Embassy in Tokyo. The Japanese military police were most unpleasant and overbearing during my return trip.

I was assistant naval attache from April 1937 until March 1939. The Japanese government had already denounced the Washington Arms Treaty and the London Arms Treaties and announced they were no longer bound by their conditions. A report came out of Italy that Japan was building three super-battleships of 45,000 tons each with 18-inch guns,

I asked a friend of mine, who had some contacts with the Japanese in official circles, to see if he could determine whether or not this story was planted in Italy by the Japanese. The reaction wasn't what I had expected. They didn't say "No, we didn't plant it" nor show any interest in the Italian story at all. This, in view of Japanese secrecy concerning all naval construction plans, was somewhat strange, I thought.

Eventually Washington asked us to officially seek the Japanese Navy's comment on this matter. Captain Bemis and I went down to the Navy Ministry and put this question to the naval liaison officer, who said he would ask his superiors for the reply and furnish it when it had been prepared. The Japanese navy's reply was a masterpiece of saying nothing in Japanese. It denied, in an indirect way, "The basis of the speculation in the Italian press over matters of no concern to the Italians." Captain Bemis said he didn't understand it, "did their reply say the report had no basis in fact?" The liaison officer said, "No, I said it has no foundation, no basis." To Captain Bemis' question, "What do you mean it has no basis?", he said, "Well, whatever we are building is a secret; only those in the highest places of authority in Japan know what we are building. I, myself, do not know; so how can anyone write a story in Italy when they don't know; therefore it had no basis."

Q: So you knew actually after all this go-around that the story was true, didn't you?

Layton #1 - 65

Layton: No, I didn't. They could be building something quite different and still tell you this, so you wouldn't know what they were actually building. The British had reports well before Pearl Harbor that the Japanese were building pocket battleships (like the _Deutschland_). Other reports said that they were building super-cruisers with small flight-decks forward in place of turrets. None of these latter reports were true. The 18" gun-superbattleship was true.

Q: Then our next segment or section becomes your return to the United States in April 1939 when you became commanding officer of the destroyer, the _Boggs_.

Layton: Nothing of note while I commanded the _Boggs_, except I got orders as Intelligence officer on staff of CinC U.S. Fleet in November 1940.

I was detached in Pearl Harbor on Saturday, December 7, 1940 and reported immediately on board the USS _New Mexico_ which was then flagship of Admiral Joe Richardson, CinC U.S. Fleet.

Q: Can you tell me anything about your experiences with Admiral Richardson? What was your job with him?

Layton: Intelligence -- Fleet Intelligence Officer. I have already told you of making contact with Rochefort's Communicating Intelligence Unit at Pearl Harbor, and working on the development of the intelligence of the Japanese militarization of the Mandated Islands.

Q: But I was curious to know before Admiral Richardson left, did you have any particular anecdotes or relationships which we want to discuss-between you and Admiral Richardson?

Layton: I liked him very much. He was very forthright and direct. Shortly after I reported aboard, Admiral Nomura was to pass through Honolulu enroute to Washington as Japan's new Ambassador to the U.S. I had known Admiral Nomura years before; at his personal request I had tutored his son's friend (his God-son) in English conversation for his Foreign Office examinations. Admiral Richardson asked me to be Admiral Nomura's honorary aide for the day that he was in Honolulu. I met his ship at the dock when it came in and acted as his naval aide during his stay. I accompanied him on his official calls, receptions, and to a big dinner given in his honor by the Japanese in the Hawaiian Islands. I was the only non-Japanese and they obviously didn't expect me there.

After being introduced, he made a speech in Japanese, in which he said, "I won't have to have this talk interpreted because "Leftenant" Commander Layton understands Japanese perfectly. I want you to know that he's an old friend of mine. He's here as my personal guest and as my friend. I am going as ambassador to Washington; I am going there to make friends and straighten out any problems our nations may have.

I want my old friend "Leftenant" Commander Layton here to be present during all my conversations and all speeches I make here, because I have nothing to hide from anyone, and I want him to know and assure his government that I am sincere and honest." I saw him several times in Tokyo before he died there in 1965; speaking of his days as Ambassador he'd say: "You know, in America they'll never understand or believe that I never knew about Pearl Harbor."

Q: Did you realize when Admiral Richardson was going to Washington why he was going?

Layton: No, but I think there was a Drew Pearson kind of a story out of Washington saying that he had differed with the President. I saw several dispatches in which he wanted to send ships back to the West Coast so they could have some leave, liberty, recreation, and some overhauls; that Pearl Harbor was not a good place to keep all the Fleet; that it was very bad for morale.

Q: He was detached rather summarily by Roosevelt.

Layton: Yes.

Q: Kimmel came in February.

Layton: Sometime in February of '41.

Layton #1 - 68

Q: Now I'd like to have you tell me in some detail about your relationship with Admiral Kimmel and the activities, anecdotes, episodes that happened up to Pearl Harbor.

Layton: Admiral Kimmel was a very forthright officer. He could sometimes be a little starchy, but he was more starchy with senior officers who were lax, than with Junior officers. He was demanding in devotion to duty, setting in his own performance an outstanding example. He had little tolerance for laziness or indecision. He had an infectious, warm smile when pleased by something and a frosty demeanor, if displeased.

After he had assumed Command he sent for me to review the current intelligence and to discuss the Japanese navy, its activities, and dispositions. He wanted a full briefing on intelligence, how much we did know and how much we didn't know; I told him everything that I knew, without reservation. He wanted to know if I thought we would continue to get significant decrypts. I said, "I don't know where we are right now with regard to progress. I have not had any information other than what I picked up by talking to Rochefort, but he's not working on any system right now; his unit works in accordance with orders from Washington. We were not receiving anything then; Washington may have great quantities of information, holding it to furnish us when the time comes. An example shortly appeared to bear out this line of reasoning. At the time the Japanese moved into Indo China, CNO sent us two messages which were obvious decrypts of Japanese messages which said

Layton #1 - 69

that carrier division 2 was operating off IndoChina to back up what was virtually a Japanese ultimatum to Vichy-France and set forth the conditions to be settled in IndoChina between Siam and French IndoChina and providing for Japanese use of French air bases in French IndoChina. The receipt of these messages made us feel sure that when something important came, we would get it, particularly any messages that had a relationship to the mission of the Pacific Fleet.

Q: You said you received two.

Layton: Two at that time, yes. Later on, we were furnished a few more by CNO. This was shortly before the Pearl Harbor attack when these few messages came we believed that they were all CNO had. Furnishing us a few (of the many CNO had) made us believe that we had the whole story; it's really worse than giving you none. Among those CNO furnished us were one or two saying the Japanese were burning their codes in Batavia, Singapore, Manila and other such places none of which indicated anything other than possible trouble in SE Asia. We received the "WINDS" message too, and set intercept watches but heard nothing further. They did not send Kimmel the decrypts ordering the Jap Consul General in Honolulu to divide Pearl Harbor into zones in order to facilitate reporting the locations of U.S. naval vessels there, or the orders to him to report each day thereafter, whether there was any departures or arrivals at Pearl Harbor or not; decrypts of that nature, which should have directed CNO's eye toward Pearl Harbor were never sent to Kimmel. They had this material back there in Op-20G; it was circulated in Washington and they should have sent it to CinC Pacific Fleet! Their post Pearl Harbor excuse that they couldn't send it out to us for security sake is a bunch of hog-wash. They had sent the same kind of decrypts to us before, and sent a few before Pearl Harbor, including the famous "Winds Message". Why was it more dangerous to send in November than it was in say April or May? The very fact that CNO did send us some decrypted messages in November and early December 1941 destroys completely Washington's contention that they couldn't send the material due to "security reasons".

Q: But they were absolutely not keeping you advised.

Layton: They were not. That's been proven time and time again. It's just beyond anyone's understanding. This is why I feel that Admiral Kimmel was so badly used, so badly treated!

Q: Wasn't Rochefort's outfit breaking anything? Weren't they doing any decrypting? Weren't they keeping you informed?

Layton: No, decrypting, of the type of messages I've spoke of was not their assignment. Washington (Op-20G) gave the work assignments. Rochefort's unit was assigned cipher and code recovery for a naval system and was furnishing Kimmel with a daily Japanese naval traffic analysis. What I have been speaking of were entirely diplomatic decrypts. This is this

"Magic" referred to throughout the Pearl Harbor hearings; which Op-20G did not furnish Kimmel, as I've said.

Q: But didn't Rochefort see it?

Layton: No, he didn't get it either. Cavite had it; Admiral Hart and General MacArthur received it from Cavite. The British had it. CNO (Op-20G) had furnished the British with the machines to do this with. The machine which was supposed to have been furnished to Pearl Harbor to Rochefort's unit, went to the British. I've heard this was on the President's initiative after a meeting with Churchill.

Q: Had his unit had that machine do you think there would have been any different results?

Layton: No doubt at all! We, at Pearl Harbor were the ones who first saw the militarization starting early in 1941 in Mandated Islands - in the Marshalls, the Marianas, and the Carolines. Washington didn't notice it as I've explained before. I'm sure that had we seen messages that had to do with Pearl Harbor (like dividing the harbor to facilitate Jap reporting on our fleet there) then there would have been a different evaluation of those items of intelligence. There's an old indian saying that says the snake in your corner is the largest. This is true in intelligence. If you get intelligence that has to do with where you are, you get its importance and realize its significance. Washington, in the late autumn of 1941, was too involved with the shipping war in the Atlantic to take proper notice of the intelligence that related to the Pacific - specifically, Pearl Harbor.

Q: And your comment is that had the machine been made available to Pearl Harbor that there would have been a completely different result.

Layton: No doubt of it in my mind; this is not Monday-morning quarterbacking. We had proven that we noticed things that involved Kimmels area when Op-20G hadn't; had MAGIC decrypts been available to us, it would have, at least, alerted us to the possibility of an attack on Pearl Harbor. I had given Admiral Kimmel a translation of a part of a book (written in Japanese) entitled "Shall America and Japan fight?" I had read the whole book and had translated significant chapters that dealt with the questions in the mind of the U.S. Commander-in-Chief of the Pacific Fleet. These questions were: on declaration of war, will he move the Fleet from its West Coast bases at San Pedro and San Deigo to Pearl Harbor? Will Japanese submarines contest the Fleet's passage there? Will he have enough escorts? While the Fleets in Pearl Harbor, what is the chance of a Japanese raiding squadron, centered around a couple of Akagi class carriers, some speedy battle cruisers, such as the Haruna and Kongo, and some heavy cruisers of the Nachi class, making a raid on Pearl Harbor? This fast-stepping group can outrun, can out-gun, any American forces that might seek to interfere with their mission. Will a raiding force strike the U.S. in the Aleutians, or even occupy strategic places up there? These, said the book are a few of the concerns of the U.S. Commander-in-Chief at Pearl Harbor. As I said, I had given this summary to Admiral Kimmel to read: When he returned it we discussed the various points made by the author, in a general way. In discussing the authors idea of a Japanese carrier task force raid on Pearl Harbor, Admiral Kimmel asked me if I thought the author was writing from any official or semi-official point of view. I said hat, in view of the Japanese mania for secrecy, I doubted the author was reflecting an official position. He asked me if I thought they would take such a risk. I replied that taking such a risk would be possible, particularly if they thought they could get away with it, pointing out they were not entirely orthodox." He then sent for Captain McMorris, his head of war plans, and he said (I can almost quote this), "Sock, Layton here and I have been discussing the chances of the Japanese making an attack on us here."

He says, "What's that?"

"We were discussing something that was written in Japanese about a Japanese carrier task force making a strike on Pearl Harbor. Do you think there would be a chance of that?" McMorris replied, "Well, maybe they could, maybe they would, but I don't think so. Nope. Based upon my studies, it is my considered opinion that there are too many risks involved for the Japanese to involve themselves in this kind of an operation."

I was excused. Whether they continued to talk about that, or something else, I don't know. This matter is in the record of the Pearl Harbor investigation.

The Saturday before the Pearl Harbor attack, the 29th of November I arrived late at the wardroom mess for lunch. During lunch someone asked me my opinion of "the situation" and I replied that while I didn't know what others present might think of it, I thought that I'd be back in my office the next day (Sunday). They doubted that the situation was that serious but I repeated my conviction. On Monday, 1 December - at lunch there was a great "Ha. Ha. Ha! What happened to your crisis, Layton? Layton and his Sunday crisis." On Saturday, the 6th of December I was again late for lunch. Admiral Kimmel had sent me out to Admiral Pye aboard the California, the flagship of the Battle Force, with a dispatch reporting sightings of a concentration of transports, and naval vessels including submarines heading south of Camranh Bay and some other Japanese ships headed toward the Gulf of Siam. Admiral Pye and his acting Chief of Staff were on the quarterdeck; I handed them the message saying Admiral Kimmel would appreciate Admiral Pyes comments, if any. They both read it over and said that the Japanese were probably going to occupy a position in the Gulf of Siam as an advance base and operate from there, probably against the Burma Road. They asked me what Fleet Intelligence thought of it. I replied that I didn't believe they'd stop there, although part of their operations might be against the Burma Road. I said that I believed that they have objectives further south, probably Netherlands oil, since we've cut off our oil to them. I added that I didn't think the Japanese would leave the Philippines on their flank; that since Japan never left its flank exposed, they'd attack the Philippines, and we'd be at war.

Pye and Smith both said, "Oh, no. The Japanese won't attack us. We're too strong and too powerful."

On returning, I reported to Admiral Kimmel and related their remarks and what they had asked me, and what I had replied and their views thereto. Admiral Kimmel said, "I want you to repeat that again." I repeated it.

He looked at me in the way he could look--right straight through you --and he snorted, as if disappointed in their reply. So I went to the mess wardroom mess for lunch and apologized to the senior officer, Captain Kitts for being late I said that I'd been sent by Admiral Kimmel to Admiral Pye with the dispatch he'd seen that morning, reporting the Japanese concentration of ships in the Gulf of Siam.

During lunch several officers asked me what was the significance of the Japanese troop transports heading toward the Gulf of Siam, I repeated my belief that the Japanese wouldn't leave the Philippines on their flank, and that therefore we'd probably be at war the next day.

Captain Kitts said, "Ah, Layton and his Saturday crisis."

The following morning when I came rushing into the Headquarters building during the attack by the second wave of carrier planes, the first person I encountered was Captain Bill Kitts. He said, "Here's the guy we should have listened to more often." Later that morning Captain McMorris sent for me and I went to his office in the War Plans section. He said, "Layton, if its any satisfaction, you were right and I was wrong." I replied that I found no satisfaction in it.

Q: It didn't do any good then. Did you not have any other sources of information than Washington? You say that Rochefort wasn't working on the messages -- the decrypting of the messages. Did you have any other way to get intelligence from the Embassy in Japan, from . . . ?

Layton: That would have to come to Washington, then to us.

Q: There was nothing which you received direct.

Layton: No. Previously, I had written to my opposite number in ONI, Commander Arthur McCollum, telling him that Admiral Kimmel and I had been discussing intelligence, what we had, and what we didn't have, and what we would like to be assured of receiving, referring specifically to "DIP", meaning diplomatic, "decrypts." This was later on called "Magic" in the Pearl Harbor investigation. The letter stated that lately we hadn't been receiving any, and the situation was getting kind of tense; we thought we ought to be receiving some, or was there a "blackout" on it?--or had they "lost" their source?--(i.e., were no longer reading it?).

His reply, which is in the record of the Pearl Harbor investigation, was to the effect that they couldn't furnish us the material, because of security and also were we to receive all of the material they received, we'd have to have as big an organization as they have to analyze it. His letter concluded by stating that we had to depend on those in the Office of Naval Intelligence to go through all this material, sift it all out, and furnish us with anything that will effect the mission of Admiral Kimmel's command. I was disappointed in McCollum's reply, giving the ONI position and showed the letter to Admiral Kimmel and voiced my concern. He wrote to Admiral Stark to request assurance of intelligence support and received a similar answer. These letters are in the Pearl Harbor investigation record. Despite asking for it, and not getting it, you can still hear it said that Kimmel got "all the information", and therefore was at fault, when in fact he didn't get the intelligence and wasn't at fault. The ONI manual, ONI 11, that was in effect then clearly set forth the duty and responsibility of CNO (Director of Naval Intelligence) to keep the Commander-in-Chief of a Fleet fully apprised of all intelligence pertinent to that command. That, in my opinion, was the reason that all of that section of the ONI manual, ONI-11, was deleted - with no new instructions substituted therefore, later on during the war --- in anticipation of a post-war investigation of Pearl Harbor.

Q: What was your relationship with Admiral Kimmel?

Layton: Very satisfactory. He established a routine of a daily intelligence briefing, during which we would discuss anything he wanted to discuss. He would also send for me whenever he wanted to ask questions, or discuss international developments particularly related to the Pacific. I learned that he could ask you some very pertinent questions. He was a man of action, too.

Q: There were, of course, Japanese spies in Pearl Harbor.

Layton: All over; There were more than a hundred Japanese consular agents throughout the islands, who reported to the Consul General. There also was a member of the Consulate General (we didn't know about until after the war), an ex-naval officer, undercover, false name and all, who had been sent there by the Japanese navy to make the reports on the U.S. Navy and Pearl Harbor. He wrote his story for the Naval Institute _Proceedings_ about "I Was a Spy at Pearl Harbor."

Naval Intelligence (the District Intelligence Officer, 14th Naval District - including all the Hawaiian Islands and Pearl Harbor) were on the alert for a Japanese spy or spies, as was the G-2 of the Hawaiian Department and the FBI, but none were uncovered before Pearl Harbor.

Q: Your relationship with Admiral Kimmel, then, was such that you really had his ear. You could go directly to him. Now in your relationship with Admiral Nimitz, you were a lieutenant commander again on a new staff with him -- what was your relationship with him. Was it as easy for you to go to him, did you have his ear to the extent that you did with Admiral Kimmel?

Layton: When Admiral Nimitz first came and I had my first chance to talk to him, I asked to be detached, and to have a relief assigned; I told him I wanted to go to sea in command of a destroyer, if possible and kill Japs. He told me that he wanted me to stay on; that he had confidence in me and that I could kill more Japanese sitting in my chair on his staff, than I ever could kill by commanding a destroyer. He said that good intelligence was vital to a good estimate of the situation and to sound decisions. As he saw it, he said, operations intelligence, will be most important and that's where you can be of greatest value. I want you to be the Admiral Nagumo (the Chief of the Japanese Naval General Staff) on my staff, where your every thought, every instinct, will be that of Admiral Nagumo's; you are to see the war, their operations, their aims, from the Japanese viewpoint and keep me advised what you (as a Japanese) are thinking about, what you are doing, and what purpose, what strategy, motivates your operations. If you can do this, then I think you will be able to give me the kind of information I need for the prosecution of my mission.

Layton #1 - 80

Q: Let's go back to Kimmel, because I want to ask you again about your personal relationship with Admiral Nimitz but I do want us to get back to Admiral Kimmel; One question I wanted to ask you -- because the books say -- I want to ask your opinion -- some of the books imply that Roosevelt did know and knew that the information was in Washington and deliberately did not let it go to Pearl Harbor. I am sure you have a feeling on that subject.

Layton: I don't know. It would be hard to believe that Roosevelt himself made that decision. I really think the failure to give Pearl Harbor much of the information was due to the initial mistake they made in furnishing this Purple cipher machine scheduled for Rochefort's unit, this "Magic" machine, to the British. For example, at the end of the war, Admiral R.K. Turner asserted that Kimmel had all the information, including "MAGIC", that Washington had. He had so testified in early investigations of Pearl Harbor (Hart, Naval Court of Inquiry, Army Court of Inquiry, etc.) He had _believed_ that the decision to send the cipher machine to Rochefort's unit had been carried out and didn't know that said decision was revoked, and the cipher machine furnished, instead, to the British. Well, when the Pearl Harbor investigation came along, he looked up that facts and found out that he was wrong. I think others in Washington also thought Pearl Harbor had it automatically. The decision to give the "Purple" cipher machine to the British was, I believe, involved in trading the

U.S. secret solutions to the Japanese Deiplomatic machine cipher for the British solution to the Nazi German naval machine cipher used in submarine warfare.

Q: One would think so, however, in that kind of critical situation one shouldn't assume anything.

Layton: Now it was Roosevelt's decision to give this to the British, there's no doubt about that; thus overriding a CNO decision to send it to Pearl Harbor. It is reliably reported that he said no, give it to the British; give Pearl Harbor the next one you make. But, they never gave Rochefort's unit such a machine; the next machine they manufactured in Washington they kept there.

Q: Not that, but that Roosevelt knew in the very end that there might well be this attack on Pearl Harbor.

Layton: There isn't any doubt in my mind, if you read the congressional Pearl Harbor testimony. On the evening of 6 December 1941, a watch officer from CNO (Op-20) named Schultz, Lieutenant Schultz, carried the "MAGIC" decrypts/translations of Japan's final note (that was to be delivered the next day) to the President. He was in his sitting room upstairs with Harry Hopkins. The President read the "MAGIC" messages all the way through, then handed it to Harry Hopkins. Harry Hopkins read them and handed them back to the President, saying "what do you think?" The President said, "This means war." Schultz's testimony was that he can't remember the exact words, but there was then a discussion as to anything we could do. The President said no and then launched into a statement that we had had an honorable record and that we hadn't ever attacked anyone before and that they'd have to strike the first blow, or words to that effect. There's no doubt in my mind that the President recognized the Japanese reply as meaning war; he knew it was coming but I don't think that he gave any more thought than CNO did to the chances of an attack on Pearl Harbor.

Kimmel didn't have this "MAGIC", or many hundreds of other "MAGIC" decrypts that Washington and Cavite and London all had and which CNO did not furnish him. That's why I say that Admiral Kimmel was very badly treated and arbitrarily made the "fall-guy" for Washington's incompetent handling of intelligence involving the national interest.

Q: What was your relationship with the Combat Intelligence Unit under Admiral Kimmel? How did you work during those days?

Layton: Admiral Kimmel did not have a Combat Intelligence Unit (Communications Intelligence Unit under Rochefort) assigned to him. It was assigned to Commandant 14 Naval District to carry out functions assigned by CNO (Op-20) who also directed their line of work. CNO (Op-20) instructions, called RIP 3 (Radio Intelligence Publication 3), restricted the people who had access to this unit for liaison to the Commanders-in-Chief of the Fleets, their War Plans officers, Fleet Communications officers and Fleet Intelligence officers, and such other officers as CNO might specifically designate. So I was authorized as Fleet Intelligence officer, to establish contact and maintain a liaison with Rochefort's unit on behalf of the Commander-in-Chief Pacific Fleet.

Q: What was he then? A commander or a captain?

Layton: A lieutenant commander. We had been personal friends since we first met enroute Japan in 1929 as language students. I think that he phoned me and asked me when I was coming over to see him, shortly after I'd reported in as Fleet Intelligence officer to Admiral Richardson. So I went over and thereafter frequently. We had a special "sound-powered telephone" (no switchboard) installed for ordinary telephone liaison and later had a "scrambler" telephone installed for day to day, 24 hour liaison. Joe would always give me a brief rundown of anything new they had. Later on, I took up Kimmel's concern regarding being kept up to date. There was nothing Joe could do here because he was not working on any current systems. He was not kept advised by Op-20 as to what "Magic" they had in Washington; they didn't give that to Rochefort's unit either. He did establish a daily summary of "highlights" gleaned from traffic analysis of Japanese naval radio traffic, which was helpful but, due to its nature, was couched in non-specific terms, as a rule. I was not supposed to work in Joe's shop. However, our close relationship enabled me to know generally what he was doing, and what--if any finished intelligence was available. He allowed me to see all of reports of intercepts from Guam and Cavite, that had to do with the re-militarization of the Mandated islands, the "WE" enciphered address messages and the like.

Q: He told me and I asked him if I should ask you about it -- so this is not betraying a confidence -- that he feels he is responsible for Pearl Harbor.

Layton: Well, he's not. That's my firm opinion.

Q: He goes on the concept that the intelligence officer -- at least the job which he had -- is to tell your boss what's going to happen tomorrow and because he didn't do that that he was blameworthy.

Layton: That is the ideal; my job was the same -- to tell Admiral Kimmel in advance what was going to happen. However, the Supreme Boss, the Chief of Naval Operations, had established a mechanism for the development, processing and distribution of intelligence to his Commanders, who were our bosses. We were part of this mechanism, this system. We were also victims of it: "For want of a nail, the shoe was lost, for want of a shoe, the horse was lost, for want of a horse the rider was lost." When they asked me in the investigations of Pearl Harbor was I surprised when they attacked Pearl Harbor I said, "Yes," but I wasn't surprised that we were at war.

Q: You were not surprised that something happened at that time but you were surprised that it happened where it did.

Layton: That expresses it.

Q: Did Admiral Kimmel ever ask you your appraisal of the Japanese intentions specifically other than the description you have already given me about just in general?

Layton: I think the discussions were rather general, rather than specifics; you see, there was nothing to indicate any specific courses of action, except they are moving to the south, with an aggressive intent, we thought. We discussed that they would probably establish an advance base from which they would operate land-based aircraft to cut the Burma Road. They had said that they are going to stop all the traffic to Chiang Kai Shek and cut the Burma Road. We knew they had an intrigue in Thailand here again, you see, just before Pearl Harbor -- a week before Pearl Harbor -- CNO sent us the contents of a decrypted Japanese diplomatic message from Bangkok to Tokyo outlining their proposed course of action to entice the British to cross the border from Malaya into Siam. The Siamese would then declare the British aggressors.

Layton #1 - 86

The Japanese would then land in Southern Thailand at Singora, (where incidentally, they did land their first forces) which had an airfield ∧ From there Japanese forces would cut in and
(near the beach.)
throw back the British, "at the request of the Siamese." Prime Minister Phibun of Siam had given his assent to this plan, the message said. Here they were giving us a recent "MAGIC" decrypt telling what was going to happen down there; our eyes were already focused on that area. At this same time CNO did not furnish us with "MAGIC" decrypts (available to CNO at that same time) dealing with Pearl Harbor, like reporting our fleet there, or the orders to report the ships in Pearl Harbor each day, whether there were movements or not!

These MAGIC decrypts on the Siam plot, on the Winds Messages, the code burning messages etc, gave us the impression that CNO was furnishing us all they had that were pertinent to the Fleet Commander's mission. How wrong we were, we did not discover for more than a year!!

Q: Some place I read that Admiral Kimmel asked one of his officers on his staff, it could have been you, about where the Japanese fleet is specifically and the statement to him was, we really don't know. Then his comment, "You mean they really could be coming around Diamond Head."

Layton: From about mid November onward, Rochefort's Daily Japanese naval radio traffic analysis reports reflected a formation of various "task forces". Since these were composite forces, Admiral Kimmel told me on the 1st of December that he wanted to have a report setting forth the locations of the Japanese fleet units. Since we had no "Japanese naval "Magic", we were dependent on the Daily Fleet Traffic Analysis. I discussed this requirement with Rochefort and his officer in charge of the traffic analysis. Previously, this traffic analysis had given good general information on the movement of forces, but the Japanese navy had changed call signs on 1 November and again on 1 December. This tended to obscure the information, although we could still get some fairly good indications. At that time many fleet units were changing their locations, as seen by traffic analysis. By the time I'd prepared the report for Admiral Kimmel, Joe phoned to say more changes were being made and could I postpone that report one more day so it would reflect the latest locations?

    I told Admiral Kimmel's aide, Ernie Blake, that the material the Admiral wanted was changing all the time and that I'd have a much more meaningful report if the Admiral could allow me one more day. The reply was in the affirmative. So I told Joe to work all that night if necessary and get this thing to me first thing in the morning so I could review it before giving it to the Admiral. Even as I was reviewing it early the 2nd of December, Joe called with new changes. I made alterations and additions in pencil but did not list Carrier Divisions one, two, three, four or five, because there was no traffic (or traffic analysis) to or from the carriers or their commander nor were they the information addresses on any messages except a supply-type message to the <u>Akagi</u>. Before taking the location sheet to the admiral, I called Joe again and he said there hadn't been any information on carriers for a long time, therefore didn't know where they were, but believed they were probably in home waters. So I wrote down "unknown -- home waters?", and took the report to the Admiral. He read it through, very carefully, then said, "What! You don't know where the carriers are?" And I said, "No, sir." He said, "You haven't any idea where they are?" I said, "No, sir. That's why I have home waters down there with a question mark. I don't know."

He said, "You mean to say that you are the Intelligence officer of the Pacific Fleet and you don't know where the carriers are?" And I said, "No, sir, I don't."

He said, "For all you know, they could be coming around Diamond Head, and you wouldn't know it?" I said, "Yes, sir. But I hope they'd have been sighted by now." He kind of smiled and said, "Yes, I understand." His manner during this exchange was jocular, in that he was impressing me with the fact that I didn't know where the Japanese carriers were - and since I didn't know, they could be almost anywhere -- even rounding Diamond Head, for all I knew.

Q: I was very interested to have your comments about Rochefort's statement that he felt to blame.

Layton: I think that's a put-on; no one can doubt his sincerity but he may feel that if he'd undertaken work that was <u>not</u> assigned to him and <u>was</u> specifically assigned to Op-20G, maybe he'd have uncovered information like Op-20G had that "Pointed" to Pearl Harbor, and could have given warning, even if it cost him his job. Had he been running Op-20G and the Communications Intelligence work before Pearl Harbor, it would have been a different story, I feel sure. After the war, a person who had been in Op-20G before Pearl Harbor told me that just before the Pearl Harbor attack they had partially translated a message from the Jap Consulate General in Honolulu saying that there are no barrage ballons and no antisubmarine nets around the fleet at Pearl Harbor. This was translated, according to the record of the Pearl Harbor Investigation on Monday, 8 December. I looked into this story and found out that a new translator, a lady, had done this translation. I saw her later and she told me she had a readable, understandable translation of it on the 6th, Saturday. It was received (intercepted) on the 5th Friday, our date. She said that Kramer had put her work sheet to one side, saying that it wasn't a complete translation. I asked him about it during the latter part of the war and he said, "Yes, we had that message--but we didn't get to it in time." That's all he'd say. I also heard from another person who confirmed that the translation, including the words "barrage balloons" and "anti-torpedo nets/baffles" was available on 6 December but was apparently overlooked in their interest in the "14-part Japanese" reply in "Magic," and the "Pilot Message" directing the delivery at a specific time on Sunday, 7 December.

Had Joe Rochfort been working on those things, he would have picked that message out of all others and would have called me up and said "I've got something here your Boss will want to know . . . this guy Kita (the Consul General) is telling Tokyo that you haven't got any barrage balloons or antisubmarine baffles installed in Pearl." He would have added, "I'm going up to tell my Boss now."

Q: The difference of a person at the right time or the lack of a person at the right time is a frightening thing in history, isn't it?

How would you appraise Admiral Kimmel had he had to fight the war?

Layton: An aggressive, dynamic leader.

Q: But your relationship with him was a very nice, easy, good one.

Layton: Yes.

Q: Can we go to the point now of Pearl Harbor, which of course is a painful thing and has been covered many, many times. But you were there at such a marvelous vantage point. Can you tell me about your experience? What happened at this point of chaos from your viewpoint as at that time relatively junior in the scheme of all the admirals?

Layton: Well, I've told you most of it about "Layton and his Saturday crisis" - trauma at the mess table the Saturday before Pearl Harbor and the Saturday before that. I told you about taking the dispatch to Admiral Pye for his evaluation for Admiral Kimmel.

Q: But I mean Sunday morning right after the attack or where were you at the time of the attack.

Layton: I was in my house out beyond Diamond Head. The phone rang and it was one of the men who had the duty. He said, "The Japs are attacking. Come back immediately." I said "I heard you, the Japs are attacking, I'm coming immediately." I could hear the sounds of a machine gun firing. The moment I hung up, the phone rang again; it was Paul Crosley, the flag secretary to Admiral Kimmel, who lived next door. He said, "I'm leaving in about two minutes and Betty (his wife) is driving. Do you want a ride?" I said, "Yes, I'll be out by the mail box." I threw on some clothes and ran out to the highway just as they drove up. As we neared Honolulu, a highway patrolman pursued us with his red light on. I was in the "rumble seat" and I yelled out, "The Japs are attacking Pearl Harbor. We are on the Commander-in-Chief's staff, please keep your light on and clear the path for us to Pearl Harbor." He put on his siren and we went right straight through Honolulu, more cars falling in behind us as we progressed toward Pearl Harbor, arriving about 8:20 A.M. Another attack wave was bombing and sounds of anti-aircraft fire from the fleet could be heard.

I went to my office; my yeoman, who had had the duty gave me an intelligence log sheet, a recording of events and times, up to the minute. It included a list of the ships that had been hit, those that were sinking, those that were asking for assistance, etc., it made one physically ill! The phone rang and it was Ham Wright over in Joe's outfit saying they'd just got a direction finder bearing -- a "bilateral" -- a two way reading, in other words (either north or south). Ham reported the D.F. bearing to be 353° or 183°, I asked wasn't there a way of knowing, didn't they have a special Direction Finder that gave "unilateral" bearings? He said, "We can't get in communication with them." (Later we found the reason was that the U.S. army took over that telephone circuit - just pre-empted it without warning.)

About this time, Admiral Kimmel came out and looked at the operations plot; I had gone down there and had laid down the two bearings on the plot. Admiral Kimmel was a little testy, because of the two bearings instead of one, and not knowing whether the enemy was to the north or to the south. He felt (and correctly, too) that intelligence should be able to tell him whether the enemy was north, or to the south. At about that time a radio message was received from one of our ships reporting that two carriers were to the south of Pearl

Harbor. Actually the report was of two <u>cruisers</u>; these were <u>our</u> cruisers, but the report was garbled and it came out as <u>two carriers</u> bearing south of Pearl Harbor. We knew we did not have any carriers south of Pearl Harbor. Later that afternoon a "plot board" from one of the Jap airplanes that had crashed into the <u>Curtis</u>, the seaplane tender, was delivered to Fleet Intelligence (per standing instructions). My examination of this "plot board" and pilots navigation sheet showed the pilot's course in with his return course also laid down to a different point. This proved, for the first time, that the enemy was definitely to the north. With the "plot board" was a temporary call sign card listing the call signs for the "Carrier Task Force Commander", the "Task Force" (collectively), for the aircraft carriers "AKAGI", "KAGA", "HIRYU", "SORYU", "SHOKAKU", and "ZUIKAKU, "Battleship Division 3" (1st Section - "HIEI" and "KIRISHIMA"), "CRUISER DIVISION 8" ("TONE" and "CHIKUMA"), "Screen Commander" ("Comdesron 1" in the Nagara") and "Screen" (collective) plus 3 submarines I-19, I-21 and I-23. Thus, by late afternoon we knew the composition of the enemy attack force. The call sign card was turned over to Rochefort's unit. Of interest, shortly after Ham Wright gave me the "bilateral bearings", Joe Rochefort telephoned and said:

"The <u>Akagi</u>, the flagship of the Carrier Force is out here."

I said, "How do you know it's the <u>Akagi</u>?"

He said, "That same ham-fisted warrant officer that uses the transmitter key as if he is kicking it with his foot is on the key now; sending a message to Tokyo.

Q: Of course, you remember how you felt -- or were you just numb all day?

Layton: Numb, but mostly sick! I was there when the <u>Arizona</u> blew up; also when the <u>Cassin</u> and <u>Downes</u> were bombed in the floating dry dock and blew up.

Q: Could you see them from your office?

Layton: Oh, yes. Our office was in the submarine base on the second floor, overlooking Pearl Harbor, the Navy Yard and Battle-ship-row.

Q: That's what I meant, were you able to see them out your window?

Layton: Yes. It was pretty horrible to see; you knew that men were dying. There was the <u>Oklahoma</u>, upside down, oil was burning on the water, and the sky a pall of black smoke; things that you will never forget as long as you live. In late morning, around 11 o'clock, some officers arrived in the operations section. Later when I went there to look at the operations plot I saw a short, slightly heavy-set officer of the grade of vice admiral, still wearing a life-jacket, his white uniform spotted with fuel oil, his face blackened by smoke or soot. His eyes were almost shut, he looked dazed as he stared off into space, not saying a word. This is the Admiral Pye, who the day before, almost 24 hours to the minute, had assured me that the Japanese would not attack us because "we were too strong and too powerful."

Q: How did Admiral Kimmel conduct himself in this circumstance?

Layton: With dignity and coolness.

Q: I am sure many people were rushing into his office . . .

Layton: People were rushing in and rushing out of the Headquarters. He was calm, collected; shocked, yes; and he looked mad -- looked mad at the Japs. He looked sad, too, because a lot of men had been killed. One had this unreal feeling, as if you were in the midst of a bad dream; it still seems like a bad dream!

Q: Did he stay in his office all day?

Layton: Yes, he was there until that night. Incidentally, he was hit in the chest with a spent machine gun bullet that cut through his white uniform and raised a welt on his chest. This happened when he stood at his window, looking out over Pearl Harbor during the second-wave attack.

Layton #1 - 96

Q: I don't know that I knew that.

Layton: He picked up the bullet and showed it to me later.

Q: Did he exclaim or make any point of it at the time or only later when he told you did you know it happened?

Layton: I wasn't present when it hit. His aide was there, Ernie Blake; later when he showed it to me, he said, "I'm supposed to turn in all captured enemy material to Fleet Intelligence according to our instructions, am I not?" I said, "Yes."

He said, "I'd like to keep this, if I may."
Then he told me how, and when, it struck him. He kept the bullet.

Q: I heard some place that at the time Admiral Nimitz took over that Admiral Kimmel was still in Pearl Harbor and stood in the background during that ceremony. Do you know that to be true or not?

Layton: Potter brought that up and I said, "No, Admiral Kimmel had left." Potter insisted that he was there. I attended the first part of the ceremony than I had to go back to my office, but am sure Admiral Kimmel had left Pearl Harbor some days previously. The second part of the ceremony was the hoisting of his flag aboard a submarine. Thereafter the official flagship of the Pacific Fleet (Admiral Nimitz's flagship), at Pearl Harbor, was always a submarine.

Q: Then continue on the chronology, will you, of how Admiral Kimmel knew he was being detached. Can you tell me the circumstances surrounding that? How soon was the first contact with Washington made with him?

Layton: I don't recall.

Q: When did you know that Admiral Pye was going to take over?

Layton: When Admiral Kimmel was ordered relieved (by an official dispatch) Admiral Pye was given temporary command until Admiral Kimmel's replacement assumed command, I saw a copy of that dispatch and went to Admiral Kimmel's office to see him but no one was there except the marine orderly. The orderly would only say that Admiral Kimmel had "retired to his quarters."

Admiral Kimmel was ordered relieved of duty after the visit to Pearl Harbor of the Secretary of the Navy, Frank Knox, and his party. Admiral Kimmel's relief was not totally unexpected. Loosing baseball teams have their manager fired. I was very sorry when Admiral Kimmel left, but I realized that this was fate. I never thought at that time that he would get the dirty deal that he received.

Q: Expand on that when you say he was treated so shabbily.

Layton: CNO ordered an official investigation by Admiral Hart. CNO then convened an official Naval Court of Inquiry, the highest investigative tool available to the naval service. The Army also ordered an Army Court of Inquiry. These were headed, and composed of admirals and generals, all with field and command experience. At these investigations, each person who might be thought guilty of any infraction, or inaction or incorrect action were named "interested parties" and were allowed to attend all the hearings, hear all the testimony, have their own counsel present, and cross-examine all witnesses. This privilege and right was accorded to General Short, General Marshall, etc., by the Army and to Admiral Kimmel, Admiral Stark, etc., by the Navy. These "interested parties" and their counsels heard all the evidence. Some learned of "Magic" for the first time. These Courts of Inquiry deliberated, and arrived at their findings, which were sent to the Chief of Naval Operations (COMINCH) who was Admiral King and to General Marshall, Chief of Staff of the Army, respectively. The findings (verdict) of both these courts of inquiry were that neither Admiral Kimmel nor General Short were guilty of any dereliction of duty, nor neglect of duty.

The findings of both courts, moreover, were that if there were any neglect or dereliction of duty, it was in Washington (Stark and Marshall) for not having furnished their respective commanders at Pearl Harbor the vital intelligence available for the execution of their respective missions.

Washington, which had publically placed the blame on Short and Kimmel, couldn't let these findings stand. Having the blame placed, where it belonged, in Washington, would also involve the prestige and position of the President of the U.S. So, to cover up, CNO and the C/S of the Army applied identical but highly unusual solutions to their quandary. Each set up a new, one-man "investigation." One-man investigations were usually the tool for minor administrative inquiries, involving small unimportant matters. But some legal "shark" discovered that

Layton #1 - 100

a one-man investigation did not have any provision for the rights of an "interested party" (accused) of being present to hear all testimony, or being represented by counsel, or having the right to cross-examine witnesses. The one-man "investigation," then, became the vehicle for the CNO and the C/S of the Army to conduct a "star-chamber" inquiry without any of the usual safeguards usually guaranteed by civil or military law.

So King ordered Admiral Hewitt to be the one-man investigating board for the Navy. A Comdr. Lt. Sonnett (USNR) was given orders to act as "counsel" (prosecuting attorney) for Admiral Hewitt. Sonnett was a clever and crack attorney in the Department of Justice: Sonnett, (who later on, as Assistant Attorney General of the U.S., put John L. Lewis behind bars) conducted all the questioning. As far as I was concerned; Admiral Hewitt only administered the oath. It soon became apparent that Sonnett's questions were lawyer's "trick" questions, in which he'd ask for a "yes" or "no" answer to a long, involved question of many parts, some not directly related. After repeatedly saying that I couldn't answer such involved questions with a simple "yes" or "no", Sonnett would continue to repeat the question, as if he'd not heard my protest. I appealed to Admiral Hewitt to have his counsel phrase his questions into simple interrogatories and stop using such trick legal questions. I protested to Admiral Hewitt that Sonnett's questions were like the famous legal trap-question. "Is it true you've stopped beating your wife?"--So that any answer is incriminating: a "yes" means you beat your wife but you've stopped it; and "no" means you are still beating her!

Layton #1 - 101

Q: What did he ask you?

Layton: Now, isn't it true that, the circumstances being "x" plus "y" equalling "z", and also in view of the fact (?) that "a" plus "b" minus "c" equals "d", that so and so came about, without regard to this and that. Please, answer "yes" or "no". Now the fact was, neither a "yes" or "no" would truthfully answer the question.

Q: I see, you just had to answer "yes" or "no".

Layton: He wanted a "yes" or a "no" - either would serve his purpose to go on with another trap-question.

Q: Did he give you no opportunity to explain?

Layton: Never. It was the same question. After I had objected to Admiral Hewitt several times, he asked Sonnett to rephrase the question but after a simple question or two, Sonnett would shift back to the same, long, involved "trap" question. I refused to answer because the question couldn't be answered in that form. I saw Sonnett after the war was over, in Washington, and he came to me and apologized at great length for being "so rough on me." I told him that I could not let an apology remove the sense of unfairness I had felt over his type of questions. He said something about "having to do his duty."

Layton #1 - 102

Q: Did he do the same thing to Admiral Kimmel?

Layton: I don't know. I don't know who else he interrogated. I did state, several times that I wanted the record to show that I had objected to those questions, to the fact that they were "trick" questions, and the fact that they were designed to entrap me. I specifically appealed to Admiral Hewitt that the record show my objections and my reasons for not being able to respond to such questions. He said "so be it," but it never appeared in the printed record. The first time I saw the record was when the Congressional Pearl Harbor investigation had commenced in early December 1945. The "one-man" Hewitt (Sonnett) investigation was in early 1945, about March when I was called back from Guam to Pearl Harbor to appear.

Q: Is this the one time then that's going to be permanent record that you are saying it now?

Layton: Yes. The purpose of that investigation was officially announced as a further investigation of matters that had not been fully covered by the Navy Court of Inquiry, or which were not entirely clear. The "interested parties" to the Court of Inquiry objected to the one-man investigation when they discovered that they could not be present, nor have counsel present, nor cross-examine witnesses. Their objections, even though perfectly proper, were ignored!

Q: It would have been so neat to have been able to blame Short and Kimmel and then close the book.

Layton: Yes but that wasn't what the Courts of Inquiry had found. Washington had to cast some doubt on the Court of Inquiry, so the Chief of Naval Operations, (COMINCH) Admiral King, and the Chief of Staff of the Army, General Marshall, ordered these "one-man" investigations, so that they could revise, and rewrite the verdict of the Courts of Inquiry. Remember, the Army Court of Inquiry and the Navy Court of Inquiry both, and separately, found Short and Kimmel, respectively, <u>free</u> of neglect of duty or improper performance of duty and found that Marshall's and Stark's performance of duty to be less than could be expected, or some-such wording. In plain words, the verdicts of these Courts of Inquiry were to find Marshall and Stark <u>guilty</u> and Short and Kimmel <u>not guilty</u> of failure to meet proper standards of performance of duty. These "one-man" investigations were merely legal frauds, with which to overturn the Courts of Inquiry.

Layton: This was the dirtiest trick; the way they treated Admiral Kimmel was disgraceful; to think the Navy would do this to their own! King may have been a great naval officer but he was, in my opinion, less that "great" when he found it politically expedient to follow the President's wishes to "white wash Washington" for the disaster at Pearl Harbor and to make a "scape-goat" of Admiral Kimmel through such shoddy legal maneuvers as that "one-man" investigation. Such an action destroyed a lot of my faith in the Navy; I just couldn't believe that such a dishonest thing could happen. This is why, you see, my sympathies are strongly with Admiral Kimmel and very bitter toward those in Washington who acted so basely.

Q: You mean Admiral King?

Layton: He was the Chief of Naval Operations and COMINCH at the time. The final "verdict" of guilt on Kimmel was signed by him. As the person responsible for that miscarriage of justice, he killed Kimmel. Kimmel died of a broken heart. Short died sometime before Kimmel, and also of a broken heart, it seems.

Q: I knew Kimmel's son and he was suffering from the tragedy of his father.

Layton: There's no doubt about it. If there is anything I can ever do to clear that record, I'll do it; that is why I have been so verbose concerning the Pearl Harbor matter, but it won't change anything. The public have been told, have read, that Kimmel and Short were wrong; they say, Wasn't it awful that these people allowed our Fleet to be destroyed and our boys to be killed?"

Q: So you stayed on and what was the timing of this Sonnett affair?

Layton #1 - 105

Layton: That was in March of 1945.

Q: Way long!

Layton: You see, The Courts of Inquiry weren't held until either late 1943 or early 1944. Their findings were then held up pending the conclusion of the Army and Navy "one-man" investigations. The Army and the Navy announced their "verdicts" (that Kimmel and Short were guilty of negligence etc.,) on V-J Day.

Q: Tell me what happened under Admiral Pye besides the Wake affair.

Layton: When Admiral Pye was acting C in C Pacific Fleet, he used his staff but depended on the war plans section of Kimmel's (Fleet) staff, but he relied on his own operations people. Of course, the relief of Wake had been planned by Kimmel (and Kimmel's staff) and the forces allocated to relieve Wake had been started by Kimmel before he was relieved. Maybe the shock of Pearl Harbor effected Pye's self-confidence. Maybe the responsibility, the chance of having our relief force attacked/ defeated may have overwhelmed him; it seemed that the minute he had an excuse to call it back, he did so.

Q: Let's see -- I forget what the excuse was?

Layton: We believed there were some Japanese carriers around Wake in support of the Wake landing. Traffic analysis suggested that Carrier Division Two may have been detached from the Pearl Harbor Strike Force to go and assist in another assault on Wake.

Q: And there were those who felt that had we gone ahead and attacked at that point it would have been a real blow at the Japanese Fleet.

Layton: Had he been successful, and caught those carriers like was done at Midway later, it would have been a real blow to the Japs as it would have been their second failure at Wake and would have taken some of their Pearl Harbor glory away. It would have been a great morale lifter for the U. S. Some said we couldn't afford to lose any carriers; we couldn't afford to lose the Saratoga, which had the Marine squadrons on board to fly to Wake and be based there. "Butch" O'Hare, who later received the Congressional Medal of Honor, told me (after the Saratoga returned to Pearl Harbor from this frustrated attempt to reinforce Wake) that the Marine fliers (who had been scheduled to go to join their fellow marines on Wake) were nearly mutinous, and some threatened to get in their planes and fly to Wake, regardless, when Pye's orders to cancel the operation became known to them.

Q: I know that when they did get back, the morale was even lower at that point, I'm told, than after Pearl Harbor.

Layton #1 - 107

Layton: It was bad! To lose to an enemy that fought you, and fought you well, is one thing, but to lose because your own admirals wouldn't take the risk, was a "Nervous Nelly," was another.

Q: Was it a matter of two weeks? Admiral Nimitz came on Christmas day as I recall.

Layton: I think he took over command the last day of December -- the 31st. It could be 30 or 31st but it was at the end of December 1941. Admiral Nimitz was there a few days before he took command.

Q: Before we go on to Admiral Nimitz, what was your relationship with Waldo Drake during the Kimmel days?

Layton: It was very cordial. I had known Waldo when he was a reporter for the Los Angeles Times covering the shipping news; he was also a naval reserve intelligence officer then. Our relations were very good and very cordial and they worked out fine throughout the war.

Q: You had spoken to me about your very pleasant and easy relationship with Admiral Kimmel and you told me also what Admiral Nimitz told you about putting yourself in the place of a Japanese naval officer but I'm wondering was your relationship as easy and pleasant and was he as easy to reach as your relationship had been with Admiral Kimmel?

Layton: Yes. I don't believe it was quite as easy at the very beginning; the war was started and it was a tense period but it was not long before an easy, informal atmosphere prevailed in my briefing him on a daily basis. I should say first that he said to me that he wanted me to be in his office at five minutes of eight every morning and later that was changed to exactly eight o'clock. I was there promptly, and we'd go right into the business of the briefing, after which he would ask questions about various things having to do with the intelligence, the war, and the enemy reactions; a whole gamut of questions. In addition to the daily briefing, I would go to his office to give him additional intelligence reports or specific bits of information on a priority basis. For example, if there was some information that was important, rather than wait until the next day I would go up and wait to see him. Very soon he gave orders to his aide, Lamar, that I was not to wait and that even if he was in conference with important people, if I said it was very important, he would receive me, excusing the important visitor while he heard what I had to report. This didn't happen very often. Once, I recall that I asked to be heard "immediately".

Q: What was the occasion for that?

Layton: I thought that was so important, time being a factor, he'd want to know right away. Just before Midway, but it turned

Layton #1 - 109

out that he had already been briefed on this by Rochefort himself -- but I didn't know this. Admiral Block had hastened over with Rochefort to give Nimitz the report that they had solved the date -- the code within a code -- and had ascertained for sure that the attack could be expected on Midway on the 4th of June.

Q: How soon after the first of the year in 1942 were you able to start reading the traffic again and be able to include the decryptions into your intelligence reports?

Layton: I don't recall exactly. There were some bits and pieces, I recall, about Japanese forces going to invade Rabaul, an operation called the "RR" Operation. I was enabled to report this to Admiral Nimitz and give him a general breakdown of the forces involved. The latter was derived from traffic analysis from Rochefort's shop. As a matter of fact, Admiral Nimitz became rather expert in understanding traffic analysis, and the special language that goes along with it. It's rather an inexact science but it has certain suggestions and hints of things that will (or might) happen; you have to tie these together, otherwise they don't make much sense. But he soon caught on to this, and was able to understand very well what it was all about.

Q: I would have thought that would make your briefing much easier.

Layton: It does but it being inexact, by nature, it can be

misleading, too.

Q: According to the books there was a so-called second attack on Pearl Harbor. Can you expand on that for me?

Layton: Yes, this is all covered in the Naval Institute Proceedings issue, I believe, of May 1953, in my article entitled "Rendezvous in Reverse." I came across some Japanese records immediately after the war, which confirmed something that we had believed to be true but couldn't prove. The second bombing of Pearl Harbor was carried out on 5 March 1942 by two four-engined seaplanes, based in the Marshall Islands; they refueled (as we had believed) at French Frigate Shoals, (to the west of Oahu) -- and as the planes approached Oahu, they were picked up on the radar and tracked for more than two hours. The air alert was not sounded until just before the bombs were dropped; the bombs hit near Roosevelt High School, nearly two miles distant from Pearl Harbor, and did no damage. The next morning there was a great hassle between the Army Air Corps and Navy aviators. The Naval Aviators claimed the bombs were dropped by some Army Air Corps plane, jettisoning his bombs before landing, and vice versa. Neither the Army nor Navy flyers gave any consideration to the possibility of enemy attacks nor the radar plots. We had noticed unusual Japanese Naval radio traffic associating the Commander Submarines and Commander Aircraft (in the Marshalls) with the Commander Forth (mandate) Fleet and the High Command. We had radio direction finder "fixes" of

Layton #1 - 111

transmissions in the vicinity of French Frigate Shoals. The unusual associations of aircraft (including seaplanes) and submarines, plus the D/F bearings suggested a Japanese bombing, by a seaplane - refuelled from a submarine and when asked by Admiral Nimitz, I gave that estimate, I reminded him that a good submarine "yarn" written by Alec Hudson, called "Rendezvous" had appeared in the August 1941 Saturday Evening Post. This story dealt with Americans refuelling PBYs (at an advanced base) from submarines and conducting a bomb attack. Admiral Nimitz remembered the story and asked if I thought that the Japanese had used that method, and French Frigate Shoals, for the bombing of Oahu early that morning, I replied that I did. Moreover, I had checked with the author, who worked (then) for Rochefort, and found he agreed, reluctantly, that such was probably the case. Shortly therafter, the Fleet Aviation Officer came to my desk, convinced that the bombs had been dropped by an Army plane, and was very dubious of my estimate of Japanese seaplanes, belittling Japanese aviation capabilities. Shortly thereafter, the Bomb Disposal Squad, which I had sent to the scene to investigate, came to my office with fragments of the bombs, and announced that they were undoubtedly Japanese bombs, similar (in many details) to some Japanese bombs that had been recovered and analyzed after Pearl Harbor. The Ordinance Inspectors mark on the tail fins matched those from the Pearl Harbor attack, also.

Q: You had known ahead of time, however, that they were coming?

Layton: Our analysis of Japanese naval radio traffic showed that something unusual was in the making. This was not specific enough to forecast an attack on Pearl Harbor, but we were conscious of something "in the wind," something brewing. However, when these unusual associations in traffic appeared again in a day or so, it was now sufficient to warn the commands of a possible reconnaissance bombing of Pearl Harbor and other bases in the Hawaiian Sea Frontier area, which included Midway, Johnston, Palmyra, Christmas Island, etc. Now warned, Midway's radar picked up two "bogies" several days later, "scrambled" Marine Corps fighter - interceptors who shot down one plane. The other got away. The one shot down at Midway had been the flight commander's plane during their attack on Pearl Harbor, the other plane took photographs of Johnston Island, which were forwarded to Tokyo with the report of these operations of early March 1942. Thus, the Japanese High Command were deprived of photographic intelligence needed in their planning for their attack (and occupation) of Midway less than three months in the future.

Again, in late May of 1942, these unusual associations of submarines, the Submarine Command, and the Commander of Patrol Aircraft in the Marshalls, the Commander of the Fourth (Mandates) Fleet and the High Command in high precedence naval traffic appeared. It was practically identical (except for different submarines) to the previous associations, and suggested another combined patrol plane - submarine - operation. With Midway's attack approaching, it suggested an armed reconnaissance, including a bombing of

Layton #1 - 113

Pearl Harbor. Since the previous attack, the second bombing of Pearl Harbor had been carried out during a full moon, the impending attack/reconnaissance would seem to "fit," conveniently, with the full moon on 30 May. However, as a result of the March seaplane-submarine operation there, Admiral Nimitz had ordered French Frigate Shoals mined; also, in preparation for the battle of Midway, auxiliary seaplane tenders and some ex-tuna boat patrol boats were stationed at French Frigate Shoals in the latter part of May. The result was when the Japanese refuelling submarines arrived off French Frigate Shoals around the 28th or 29th they reported that American ships were there; the operation was postponed for one day but when our ships were again reported as anchored at French Frigate Shoals, rendering the operation impossible, they cancelled it. I've observed that post-war Japanese historians blame their failure in the Battle of Midway to this failure to make the planned reconnaissance of Pearl Harbor in late May -- that their report of the absence of the U. S. Naval forces would have alerted Yamamoto to the trap that was set for him at Midway. I should emphasize that the intelligence concerning the early March second attack on Pearl Harbor, the mid March reconnaissance of Midway and Johnston Islands and the planned reconnaissance/attack on Pearl Harbor by Flying Boats was all derived from traffic analysis and not from decrypted enemy messages.

Q: Your DSM indicates that you assisted in all commands in

planning and conducting every amphibious campaign, fleet engagement, and carrier attack and will you describe to me how you put together and how your intelligence functioned in general. And then I would like to ask you about specifics.

Layton: Well, that's a pretty big order. No commander can plan any operation or any campaign without having the intelligence on which to base his plans. Basic intelligence, or strategic intelligence of a certain location is normally available in standard intelligence surveys or other publications. But there is never enough details; there is never enough accurate, up to date intelligence.

As an example, the mission of the Pacific Fleet, pre-Pearl Harbor and after Pearl Harbor as well, was (basically) to advance and capture a position in the Marshall Islands, from which to establish a forward Fleet base; thence to advance further, establishing advance bases, being ready meanwhile to launch an attack against Japanese main strengths.

As a result of Pearl Harbor -- and this is another side light -- Pearl Harbor and its tragedy also had its profits -- it caused the Navy to postpone this first step. First, they didn't have the strength, the carrier based air support and cover, nor sufficient amphibious strengths, nor enough intelligence to seize this "position in the Marshall Islands." Admiral Nimitz conferred with me as to how best to remedy the lack of sufficient intelligence. This resulted in his directive setting up the Intelligence Center, at Pearl Harbor, where all Naval intelligence would be collected, analysed; later when he became the Commander of the Pacific Ocean area, the Intelligence Center became a joint Army-Navy effort, renamed Joint Intelligence Center Pacific Ocean Area, "J.I.C.P.O.A." Submarine reconnaissance of Japanese strong points in the Marshall Islands and other mandated islands was undertaken in connection with the initiation of war-patrols immediately after Pearl Harbor. This periscope reconnaissance confirmed Japan's militarization of those islands, as had been discovered early in 1941 through analysis of "WE" - address encipherments. Coast Defense guns, airfields, hangars, anti-aircraft batteries, store house, radio stations and barracks were seen and reported, but <u>detailed</u>, precise information was necessary before any assult could be planned. This intelligence, confirming other intelligence (which may have been doubted by some) resulted in Nimitz's decision to carry out a carrier task force raid on these positions in the Marshall Islands, which was carried out on 1 February 1942. Although photography for intelligence purposes was urged in the orders to conduct that raid, no <u>useful</u> photography resulted, unfortunately. Thereafter. carrier task force attacks on enemy positions required that photography for intelligence purposes be carried out.

    The various strategic and Operational Planners now realized their need for photographic intelligence -- aerial photographs, oblique photographs, close-in photographs -- even submarine (periscope) photography, before any assult on the Marshalls could be done. We could not afford to risk the loss of our few aircraft carriers for such intelligence gathering missions and did not until after Midway and the destruction of Japan's main carrier strengths. Later on our preponderence of carrier strength enabled us to do so. The U. S. did not, then, have any base from which a successful aerial reconnaissance of "a position in the Marshalls" could be continued up through some future "D" - Day. So in order to get the necessary intelligence, plans were changed to acquire and build bases from which aerial intelligence could be obtained on a continuing basis. So we established bases in the ELLICE Islands, so that we could get intelligence on TARAWA in the Gilberts, assult and occupy that place and establish an advance base there from which to make the basic plan's seizure of "a position in the Marshalls." At the outbreak of war, the Japs had seized the Gilbert Islands to protect their Marshall's southern flank. They strongly fortified TARAWA, and recognized that if we recaptured the Gilberts, we would be a threat to their Marshalls bases. The Japs were confident that the U. S. war plan called for assault and seizure of positions in the Marshalls, from which to attack Japan.

Lack of accurate, up to date, intelligence on Japanese newly established bases in the Marshalls, and in the Gilberts (Tarawa), caused the revision in U. S. war plans for the Pacific. Bases for collection of current intelligence had to be set up in the Ellice Islands so that Tarawa could be taken and used as an intelligence collection base for up-to-the-minute intelligence on selected Marshalls bases. Only then could "a position" be established in the Marshall Islands."

After we captured Tarawa, Admiral Nimitz very carefully questioned me day after day because I was reporting that the Japanese were moving forces within the Marshalls almost every day. We had pretty good intelligence then. We knew that sizeable army forces had suddenly arrived in the Marshall Islands. They hadn't been there the year before. These army forces were being shuttled out of Kwajalein, the Marshalls Headquarters area, to the outward perimeter islands of Wotje, Tarawa, Mile, Jaluit and other less strongly fortified positions. These positions were being greatly strengthened with men and defensive material. Certain naval units were also being taken out of Kwajalein and moved to these outer islands. When I reported this to Admiral Nimitz, he said, "I want you to re-capitulate all of this and give me a summary of their new strengths and dispositions." We gave him a strength and disposition report for these places every week. The "order of battle" was good. They talk about counting the privy holes on the various islands of the Solomons -- we had a better way. Rochefort had discovered early in the war, the various Japanese commands were making administrative reports -- the number of rations expended, the number of sick days and deaths, on a monthly basis. Once his unit had broken through the encipherments etc., we knew at the end of the month we came to know the number of rations expended on each atoll command; divided by the number of days in the month, gave you a pretty accurate count of the number of people "on board" a given atoll or base. That "order of battle," was pretty accurate. Just before the assault on the Marshalls, I briefed Admiral Nimitz, Admiral Spruance, Admiral Turner, General H. M. Smith of the Marines etc. "Howling Mad" Smith wouldn't believe it when our figures (order of battle) showed six Japanese on Majuro. He said, "You mean 6,000." I said, "No, six." (Actually it turned out there was one. They had withdrawn the other 5. There had been a lookout station there. General Smith's interest in Majuro was because that enclosed atoll had a good anchorage and was to be seized as an advance-anchorage for the assault reserves and logistic ships. Admiral Nimitz, who knew the reasons for our "order of battle" estimates was amused.

For example, before the assault on Tarawa, we knew they had mounted four 8-inch coast-defense guns there. The photographic interpretation of the aerial photographs was recorded as four - "6 inch guns." We knew from Rochefort's unit, or Washington, that the Japs had brought in four 8 inch coast defense guns that they'd captured earlier in the war in the Singapore area.

Interview #2

Rear Admiral Edwin T. Layton, U.S. Navy (Ret.)

Subject: Biography   Date: May 31, 1970

Interviewer: Etta-Belle Kitchen, CDR, USN (Ret.)

Q: I wish you would describe to me the procedures through which you went. You were sitting in an office in Pearl Harbor and I would like you to go through the steps which you took in order to develop your intelligence for say one particular operation. Take as example Coral Sea.

Layton: That was before we had any back-up organization like the Intelligence Center or J.I.C.P.O.A. At that time, Rochefort phoned me on this special phone we had to say he had a hot one coming over and it looks like something is going to happen that the man with the blue eyes will want to know about. The man with the blue eyes, of course, was Chester Nimitz. I said, "Yes, I'll get it to him right away." He said, "I just called to alert you that it is coming over."

Very shortly there would arrive by messenger a copy of the decrypt in its actual condition of non-completion, or non-comprehension; it contained many blanks -- it would say: "so-and-so," blank, blank, blank, and "so-and-so," blank. I would call Joe and say, "Have you got any idea what these blanks are?"

He would say, "No, we don't know but we're working on

them. But I have a hunch that that first blank in there represents -- and he'd use the Japanese word -- and the second blank might be such-and-such word (in Japanese), etc. --- they might be used there and would seem to form a normal sentence, but I don;t know this." From previous experience this would be the kind of context. I think that's the kind of grammatical filler."

And I said, "Do you think the force involved is from the traffic analysis which associates Carrier Division Five and Cruiser Division Six and some spare divisions, or units and some auxiliaries?"

He said, "Yes, and we have in here a "Koryaku Butai." (which means invasion force) and there's a "M" and an "O" used to form "MO"; we know that's Moresby --- hence a "MO Koryaku Butai...." a force to assault Port Moresby. We think that's the objective."

I went up to tell Admiral Nimitz that I had something special. I said that there was an invasion force forming at Rabaul, consisting of Carrier Division Five, which was the ZUIKAKU and SHOKAKU; and Cruiser Division Six, AOBA, KAKO, the FURUTAKA, and KINUGASA; and destroyer divisions and possibly an aircraft auxiliary plus a "MARU," a merchant ship converted into a seaplane tender (--I've forgotten whether it was the KAMIKAWA or KUNIKAWA MARU). He said, "Do you know the location of CarDiv Five right now?" I said, "Well, they're not in Rabaul. I think they're around Truk but I'm not real sure."

Layton #2 - 121

Pretty soon, traffic analysis showed messages for CarDiv 5 being routed/re-routed by Truk radio down to Rabaul radio network. Such a shift in routing of Japanese naval radio traffic usually, but not always, indicated a change in the units geographic position. One could also tell from the increased intensity of aerial patrols and searches that the Japanese were starting some operation; their invasion (assault) forces had to depart before their other forces because they were slower. Our submarines, I think, also reported that there were a number of ships moving out of the Rabaul area. Fleet Intelligence U. S. Pacific Fleet had been previously directed by COMINCH to send a daily Intelligence Summary by radio to certain commands. The daily Intelligence Summary, of course, included such information and went to Admirals Fletcher and Fitch in the Coral Sea as well as Cruiser Division Commanders, Battleship and Carrier Division Commanders, to General MacArthur's headquarters, as well as to the Australian Naval Board, the New Zealand Naval Board, and COMINCH. The daily Fleet Intelligence Bulletin would not disclose the source of the information but would "estimate Japs intend amphibious assault on Port Moresby near future under cover carrier air attack by SHOKAKU, ZUIKAKU and shore based air.

After a careful study of all the bits and pieces, an assault on Port Moresby was indeed indicated. In his orders to Admiral Fletcher (and to Admiral Fitch), Admiral Nimitz would be more specific, telling them that he believed that a Japanese Striking Force, centered in the carriers ZUIKAKU and the SHOKAKU of CarDiv Five, and escorted by part of CruDiv 5 (eight-inch) cruisers, and destroyers, would cover and act as the major force for the invasion of Port Moresby; the Invasion Force, consisting of CruDiv 6 (eight-inch gun cruisers), CruDiv 18 (2 old 6" gun cruisers), about ten marus and other auxiliary ships, including converted seaplane tenders, minesweepers and subchasers and destroyers, would probably proceed through Joumard Passage, around the tail of New Guinea. The carrier forces would probably extend further to the east in the Coral Sea and cover the invasion forces by aerial strikes on northeastern Australian and Port Moresby air fields.

At about the time of the Battle of the Coral Sea, early May 1942, Rochefort's traffic analysis alerted us to a very unusual, and highly significant series of messages associating the High Command with just about the whole Japanese Navy. There was also a decrypt, full of blanks, but also including a "Koryaku Butai" (invasion-assault force), an "A" "F" "Koryaku Butai." As I recall it, "A" "F" was an unknown location, but thought to be Midway.

I went to Admiral Nimitz and told him that it looked like there was going to be an invasion of Midway by a Japanese task force; that it seemed like almost the whole Japanese Navy would participate. I said this intelligence was so important that I wanted him to have the same confidence that I had; that while the material was incomplete and full of holes, and imprecise, it was also much firmer than some of the stuff we'd had; that it had some "firm" values. It clearly indicated Japanese plans underway for a huge operation aimed toward Midway, or the Hawaiian Island area, in the near future --- one that would involve the whole Japanese Navy except the Mandate Fleet now involved in the Port Moresby operations.

I wanted Admiral Nimitz to see these pieces at first hand and urged him to do so, but he said he was just too busy; that he would believe what I said. And I said, "It isn't that. I want you to see it and be as convinced as I am. At that time the main strength of the Pacific Fleet (excepting the Battleships) was thousands of miles away, down in the Coral Sea.

We had no time or dates for the invasion of Midway, but we believed that, at that time, it could be any time around the 30th of May. He said that he would send Captain Lynde McCormick, who was his head of War Plans to look over the material on his own behalf. McCormick had been number two in War Plans before Pearl Harbor, and had become Nimitz's War Plans Officer when Captain McMorris was detached for a command at sea. I told Joe that Captain McCormick and myself were coming to see the material at first hand. Rochefort had laid out his "exhibits" on sheets of plywood on sawhorses. He didn't have enough tables or desks on which to lay out his "exhibits" -- many pieces of paper, here and there, but all inter-related, we thought.

We went over the papers, one by one; we went through the whole compilation of traffic analysis, how each command, or unit, became associated with others and then continue in association with still others, where there had been no association before; how these new associations continued to be together, how there had been general associations between commanders, but now all the ships of a division are often brought into common traffic association. It's like Virginia Reel or a square dance. Those concerned "become associated" (are participants) and thereafter follow an intricate pattern in relation, one to the other; they would nearly always "do-se-do" back with their partners, or with another "set." That's probably a silly analogy: but those most prominent in traffic associations are the dancers who dance together; commands not associated with these, or who aren't prominent in traffic rarely appear at the party (dance). Sometimes a command, or a unit, appears but once in association with the "associates"; such a unit's association is usually considered accidental and it's possible "membership" in the "association" is then eliminated. Incidently, our Midway analysis, (estimate of enemy forces), was called successful intelligence, probably since we won..... the fact was -- we didn't have Battleship Divisions 1 and 2 in our order of battle because it reflected this one-time/casual association, believed accidental. Had we lost the Battle of Midway and had the Japanese battleships come on to try to destroy the rest of our fleet, it would have been a great failure of intelligence.....the failure to have included the battleships in our "order of battle."

Q: Did Captain McCormick understand the explanation?

Layton: Oh yes. When he went back, he told Admiral Nimitz that he was a little more forcibly impressed that what I had previously said would be the course of events; that seeing the raw-material at first-hand had reinforced his own conviction of an impending invasion of Midway. He added that he had a great respect for Rochefort and the people who were doing this work.

Q: Well, eventually before Midway didn't the battle order from the Japanese become read -- the entire thing?

Layton: No. Everything that has been written about that is absolutely, unqualifiedly false.

Q: Is that so?

Layton: That's right. The people who said that are people who don't know the facts. They are wrong! Had any such full reading occurred before the battle, I'd have known of it -- Nimitz would have been told!

Q: Well, Lord says it.

Layton: I know. He got it from Safford, I'm told; I asked Lord after I'd read his book where he got that; he said that Safford told him. I replied that Safford didn't know what he was talking about. Had we been able to read the entire battle order, as has been written, we would have had the battleships in our order of battle for Midway. I didn't realize I was making a point, but that is the point.

There was no such message, as comes out in "The Code Breakers" and in Lord's "Incredible Victory" etc. It's like some other "historic accounts"—like writers who have said Kimmel was at fault.

Q: When somebody repeats it, they become involved.

Layton: They become involved. And it's the same way--I point this out for historians in the future.

Q: And the first person that says it says "I think . . ." And the next person who repeats it forgets to use the "I think."

Layton: A little lesson of history I have learned recently is that you have to be very careful of what you accept as historic accuracy. I have discovered that the same sentence, the same expression, often used by Japanese in relating (supposedly from their own experience) what happened during the war, are quotations extracted from statements in the Reports of the United States Strategic Bombing Survey.

Q: Well, we brought it out yesterday. That's why I asked you if Admiral Kimmel was in the background and you said that you believed that I was going to question you on that again today. You still feel that Admiral Kimmel had left before Admiral Nimitz took over?

Layton: I feel as sure of this as if I knew it but I don't know it. If I knew it, I'd say positively. But I am positive in my mind but I could be entirely wrong because my recollection isn't perfect, by far. But I feel absolutely sure that Admiral Kimmel left before Admiral Nimitz took over.

Q: Correct. Now the battle order which we were just discussing, to make it perfectly clear, there never was a complete battle order as is reported in some of the books.

Layton: Never was. Not available to us.

Layton: After Midway, the need for more people came up again and again. When I approached Admiral Nimitz on this subject he said that he had made a study of this; that Admiral Sims in World War I (in Queenstown) had a staff of about two hundred officers at that base. He said "I'm not going to have it. I'm just not going to have it."

I said, "Admiral, you'll have to face the facts. An effective organization must have effective support. And I, as your Intelligence Officer, cannot give you proper, or effective intelligence support unless I have enough people to do it. As the war goes on the intelligence requirements will get bigger and bigger; we must face it, you're going to have to have people to do the job."

I don't know what happened but some time later, about the time of Guadalcanal, he said he had decided that I was justified in asking for more personnel in Intelligence. I found that he was thinking in terms of only a few additional people. When I told him the need was for some forty to sixty additional intelligence personnel he said, flatly, that he wouldn't consider expanding his staff in that degree. I told him that I realized he wanted to keep his staff small, but that these additional intelligence people didn't have to be on his staff; they could be assigned ashore -- to the Naval District Intelligence Office -- especially to work for him. After discussion and further thought, he authorized the Intelligence Center, the personnel of which would be attached to the 14th Naval District. Later their organization became the Joint Intelligence Center when Admiral Nimitz was named Commander in Chief Pacific Ocean Area, a Joint Command. Before the War in the Pacific was over J.I.C.P.O.A. (Joint Intelligence Center Pacific Ocean Area) had some 1800-2000 personnel assigned to it, including "FRUPAC," a new name for Joe Rochefort's old unit.

In organizing the new Joint Staff of the Pacific Ocean Area Command, Admiral Nimitz had kept the posts of Assistant Chief of Staff Plans and Assistant Chief of Staff, Operations of the Joint Staff to be occupied by Naval officers but had promised the Assistant Chiefs of Staff, Logistics and Intelligence would be Army officers. Admiral Nimitz told me of his decisions and promises and said that while he'd have an Army Assistant Chief of Joint Staff for Intelligence, I would be his Fleet Intelligence Officer and also Combat-Intelligence Officer and Deputy to the Army man. When he told me the name of the Army officer which the Army had recommended for the post of Assistant

Chief of Joint Staff, Intelligence, I strongly recommended that he not accept him. Admiral Nimitz asked my reasons, which were: incompetance, lack of imagination, laziness and lack of professional qualifications for such an assignment.

Admiral Nimitz asked then if I had any Army officer under General Richardson's command in mind that I would recommend? I replied that there was a very competent and professionally qualified officer, who I believe'd would be an excellent J-2 and who would work out well as the head of the Joint Intelligence Center Pacific Ocean Area. That was Colonel Joseph J. Twitty, Corps of Engineers, U. S. Army, and who in the past had been the head of a mapping detachment, under General Richardson. I suggested that Admiral Nimitz ask General Richardson, personally, for Colonel Twitty's assignment for the J-2 position. General Richardson approved and Colonel Twitty, who was later promoted to Brigadier General, served as J-2 throughout the rest of the war.

Q: So you got some of the help that you needed?

Layton: Well, to make a long story short, it turned out that everyone said the Joint Intelligence Center Pacific Ocean Area (khown as JICPOA) was the greatest field organization ever in intelligence. Representatives of the Army, Air Force, Navy, Marines, Coast Guard all took part. It's strategic studies and estimates were outstanding but their field operations - their operational or combat intelligence, were simply unbelievable.

For example, when the Marines went ashore at Saipan, they landed at a place called Charon Kanoa, the Headquarters of the Japanese Army Command at Saipan. The intelligence team from JICPOA went ashore with the first wave of Marines, and by chance, occupied a schoolhouse which had been that Japanese General's command post. The Japs had just left but had failed to destroy all the documents there, so we captured all those documents.

The JICPOA team spent all night scanning and translating important documents by flashlight, under a table covered by blankets. Thus, they were able to pin-point where the Jap artillery batteries were sited and pass this word out to the bombardment force. They discovered where their tanks were dispersed and of their plans for counter-attacking our forces. When the Japs made their counterattack the first night, our people who now knew the area the tanks would come from had sighted their guns along this route, and when the tanks started assembling for the counterattack, Marine artillary went bang, bang, bang, and that was the end of the tanks, and the counterattack was cut to pieces. Their P.O.W. interrogation teams also turned out timely accurate intelligence.

This was practical application of field intelligence, combat intelligence.

Q: What about Guadalcanal? I had read or had the impression that Admiral Kelly Turner was offered an intelligence officer and because in the early days he had little regard for intelligence that he refused or didn't take advantage of this and that had something to do with . . .

Layton: Savo Island.

Q: Yes.

Layton: I don't know, first hand, of this, so I would prefer not to comment but it would fit his character, as I know it, to turn down an intelligence officer. It was said that "he was always his own Intelligence Officer."

Q: Was the traffic broken to let Turner and the people in command down there know what the Japanese forces were?

Layton: We knew, generally, the magnitude of their forces but that doesn't help you when we're up against fortifications, against beach emplacements.

Q: I mean the sea battles -- the Savo Island . . .

Layton: You're losing me. The intelligence at Guadalcanal was one thing.

Q: I don't mean the island, I mean the sea battles.

Layton: Well, there again was misuse of intelligence, and here again, intelligence itself wasn't wholly at fault. The communications, the means of passing information were deficient. Just as in the battle of Midway, progress-of-the-battle communications were not properly used. Admiral Nimitz didn't know for hours and hours that we had made the strike on the Japanese forces, or that we had hit them, or had set them on fire. Why? For the same reason that our aviators didn't know where the Japs were after their carriers had changed course; our operating people should have kept in contact and kept our carrier force adivsed as to the location of the enemy force. We had another kind of "combat intelligence unit" which had been organized by Rochefort from personnel from his communications intelligence unit. On Admiral Nimitz's authority, our senior Task Force Commanders like Admiral Spruance and Admiral Fletcher, were given a special radio intelligence unit called "Combat Intelligence Unit." Each unit consisted of trained navy intercept operators from Rochefort's unit, plus a Japanese linguist, a former Japanese language officer. These units stood intercept watches on the Japanese circuits used by their air reconnaissance and air scouting networks; they performed air "early-warning" function. During action, all tuned in their voice radios, on the enemy's air-defense commander, air-commander, and leaders of their fighter squadron, torpedo squadron, or dive bomber squadron -- (we knew the frequencies they used) and reported all activity heard, which would be passed to Admiral Fletcher, or Spruance by the language officer. The intercepted enemy voice commands to attack, or to assemble, or move further on and prepare to attack were thus made immediately available to our own

Task Force Commander, who then could make counter-moves, such as sending off more fighter interceptors, if available, and to signal his forces to "Prepare for air attack" and clear the carriers decks of refuelling, or refrain from landing aircraft. So, our Senior Task Force Commanders, like Fletcher and Spruance, knew, some minutes before the attack, that one was coming. This "Combat Intelligence Unit" became standard; we gave such a unit later to Radford, who covered the occupation and building the airfield on Baker . . .

Q: Radford?

Layton: Admiral Arthur Radford, then a rear admiral commanding a little carrier task force. After that operation he came to my office and said, "I want you to know that the "Combat Intelligence Unit" you put with me was the greatest assistance! I've never known of anything like it. I never knew any such thing existed." He said, "There I was and this young man would say to me, "Sir, there's a four-engine flying boat searching from Makin to the East --- he is now about 350 miles to the west of you coming in your direction at about 11,000 feet; at the speed he's coming, he ought to be in sight of our task force in about an hour."

Q: That must be the intelligence that was offered to Turner that he turned down.

Layton: I know he was offered one and turned it down.

Q: Now, had he had that would it have saved any . . . would it have prevented the loss at Savo Island?

Layton: Well, you see, Turner wasn't even there; he was attending a conference near Guadalcanal. Had he had such a unit in his flagship, one intercept operator would have been on duty -- just as the radar operators were. We do not know, but the chances are the intercept operator would have been monitoring the enemy surface/combat frequency. He might have searched at random on known enemy frequencies and might have picked up the scouting aircraft radio reporting in to their commander. He would have known it was the CHOKAI, the flagship of the Fleet responsible for that area. He would have heard the CHOKAI directing the scout seaplanes to drop flares to "illuminate the enemy" etc. He would have, in my opinion, gotten word to his officer-in-charge of these intercepted signals. The word of this would have been given to the Commander's deputy (since Turner was absent attending a conference). I think our forces would have been alerted, thereby. I said earlier that SAVO Island represented a misuse of intelligence. Well, this force was sighted and reported by an Australian coast watcher. At least there was a report. Then one of our planes went up to Bougainville area but when the Japanese saw this plane they turned around and went in the other direction, to mislead the plane. These reports of this force, coming from the direction they were, clearly suggested that it be carefully watched and trailed as this force represented, at a minimum, a hazard to our operations. If they viewed the enemy force in terms of a threat, then they should assume an appropriate readiness to combat that threat.

Q: Well, I just never understood how when the radio intelligence had been so excellent in the two previous occasions that one month later or two months later, that it seemed from then on for the rest of the year in the Solomons it seemed not to be effective.

Layton: Shortly before the battle of Midway the Japs changed their codes, and by Guadalcanal, the new ones had not been successfully exploited. There were no decrypts saying that the CruDiv 6 plus CHOKAI etc., will depart Rabaul at so-an-so time and proceed to Savo Island area and annihilate the American forces. Traffic analysis did not disclose the movement, probably because it was a tactical reaction to our landings at Guadalcanal rather than, as in the Coral Sea and Midway, a <u>campaign plan</u> being placed in effect, which required considerable operational and logistical arrangements.

Q: I wanted to go back to something early in '42, relating to a story which I read that CominCh sent a request directly to the Combat Intelligence Unit asking them for their appraisal of the Japanese intentions without asking Admiral Nimitz or any other command but sent it direct to Rochefort's group. In fact, Captain Rochefort says that it annoyed people

Layton #2 - 136

in Washington and perhaps some people on Nimitz' staff. Do you recall that?

Layton: I don't believe that anyone on Nimitz' staff knew of this except myself; the only reason that I learned of it was because Joe told me about it. CominCh's other hat was that of Chief of Naval Operations, commanding the naval organization and administration, while as CominCh he was the Commander-in-Chief of all naval forces. He had the same right to ask Rochefort's unit that he had to ask Safford's unit, or any unit, for their appraisal of a situation. Personally, I am inclined to think that this was a request from OP-20-G, "representing" CNO, for such an appraisal, to be used in planning future intercept facilities and personnel requirements. I feel sure that it was not a request initiated by Admiral King. He'd go to Nimitz.

Q: Rochefort felt, I believe, that during the time that Safford was in Washington that his relationships were very fine but after Safford was relieved, in fact I think about the time of Guadalcanal, that there was so much discussion and so much questioning and so much argument really with his reading of traffic that he sent a telegram or a message saying, I'm working for Admiral Nimitz and in effect, get off my back.

Layton: I think you're mistaken as to _time_. My recollection of the _time_ was that it was before Midway because that was the time when Rochefort received directions from Admiral Nimitz on exploiting specific Japanese traffic. With the Midway build-up indications increasing, there was an acute need for more precise intelligence to bear out the preliminary estimates that Midway was the objective. Around the 10th or 12th of May (roughly). I asked Rochefort "why don't you work on all messages in which Commander of First Air Fleet (their Striking Force) was an addressee, to see if a research of them will give us the data we need." He explained that under his instructions from CNO (OP-20-G) he was restricted to certain areas of Japanese naval messages and that, from an examination of the raw intercepts, many Commander First Air Fleet messages lay outside his assigned area of work. I explained the problem to Admiral Nimitz, pointing out that he had authority to divert Rochefort's unit temporarily from its assigned work-area to work directly supporting his (Nimitz's) mission and recommended that he authorize me to tell Rochefort to divert his work and concentrate on Commander First Air Fleet messages. This was done. The decrypts of these messages and the newly recovered code values and additives, were furnished CNO (OP-20-G) and other such units, as was regular procedure. CNO (OP-20-G) noticed that the messages and technical data furnished by Rochefort's unit clearly showed he was working material outside his assigned area, and "blew up" -- nasty messages being sent to Rochefort ordering him to "obey orders" and report why he was not following his instructions from CNO (OP-20-G).

Then he told them that he was operating outside his "assigned area" under direct orders from Commander-in-Chief to do so.

Layton #2 - 138

CP-20-G did not then, nor later, challenge the CinC Pacific Fleet's right to do so. But this is probably why some people in Washington knew I got the orders issued; people who knew that Joe and I were very close friends, knew we operated closely together and effectively -- and this is why they apparently felt they had to remove Rochefort and that they had to remove me also.

Q: So it was a different sequence from what I had understood it to be.

Layton: That's right.

Q: Because when they called him back there in 1942, it was in October of '42 and very soon after he had had very outstanding successes, he never returned.

Layton: Well, you see, this was part of the feud that blew up.

Q: But then why didn't Admiral Nimitz support him then?

Layton: Admiral Nimitz did. He sent a message to Admiral King saying that he didn't want Rochefort detached; that he wanted him to remain in his assignment and that he didn't want the new man who had been ordered in Rochefort's place; that he had nothing against the new man but he did not want Rochefort superceded; Nimitz's message stated that Rochefort's work had been of the greatest of value; that it actually saved the Pacific Fleet in the Battle of Midway, for example, and that Therefore he asked King's personal intervention. King came back and said, "I will do all that I can; I will cancel his orders" -- or change his orders, or words to that effect. I don't remember exactly. This was a "Personal" - King to Nimitz message that Admiral Nimitz showed to me.

I am convinced that there was a conspiracy back in Washington to get Rochefort removed. They were mad because they had insisted that the code group "AF" (actually Midway) stood for the West Coast of North America: as a result COMINCH had officially briefed General Arnold (of the Air Force) and General Marshall, that the Japanese attack that was the Battle of Midway was to be an invasion or an attack on the West Coast. As a result, before General Arnold left Washington in mid May 1942 for an inspection of his air bases, he issued orders that no heavy bombers would be redeployed without his specific authority. He had deployed his heavy bombers for the reported upcoming invasion of the West Coast. Well, when Washington CNO(OP-20-G) and, of course, COMINCH had to agree with Rochefort that "AF" (the code group for the invasion place) was Midway, they "lost much face." I can imagine Admiral King's reaction to that! It seems that they felt Rochefort had deliberately tricked them and felt they had to remove Rochefort. The fact is they did remove Rochefort, just at a time when he was most needed in the Pacific. If he'd been put in charge of Washington's (OP-20-G's) problems, a solution for the good of all would have been likely. But they did not do so.

They put him "on the shelf," temporarily.

Q: And Admiral King wouldn't support him.

Layton: I don't believe that Admiral King knew the facts! I understand that King was told that Rochefort was insubordinate, wouldn't follow directions, was uncooperative, and needed direct supervision.

Q: Then it seems to me that Admiral Nimitz didn't back him up properly.

Layton: As I said, Admiral Nimitz asked to keep Rochefort on in his assignment, that he not be transferred. Then he got a message from King saying he wanted Rochefort to come back to Washington, on temporary duty for discussions and to go over problems back there. Admiral Nimitz showed it to me and it seemed reasonable. So Rochefort was ordered back to Washington for "temporary duty." And when they got him there, his "temporary duty" orders were "modified to permanent duty." Once the permanent duty orders were issued, it was too late, you see. By the time we got a copy of those orders (by mail) it was "water over the dam."

Q: And his Distinguished Service Medal was . . .

Layton: . . . cancelled by the same clique back there.

Q: And Admiral Nimitz didn't back up his own request that Rochefort get a Distinguished Service Medal.

Layton: I mentioned this to Admiral Nimitz and pointed out that Rochefort had been spirited away over his personal protest and recommendation. Admiral Nimitz said, "Layton, I've got enough to do to fight this war. I've got other things, bigger issues. When the time comes, I hope to take those up. But right now, I can't be bothered with it."

He then showed me a personal letter he had just received from Admiral King that said, and I quote it: "Now that we have gotten rid of Rochefort, I will leave the matter of getting rid of Layton up to you."

Admiral Nimitz wanted to know who was my enemy back there? I said that I didn't know that I had any. He replied "Obviously you have" and asked "Why do they want me to get rid of you?"

Well, at that time I didn't know what was going on, and replied that I didn't know. I really didn't know -- I was dumfounded! To this day I don't _know_ what brought that about.

Shortly before the time in question, a member of the COMINCH staff sent out a Chief Yeoman to Pearl Harbor to investigate Rochefort and me.

Q: You're kidding.

Layton: I'm not kidding. I'd known this man when he was the

mail orderly on the USS WEST VIRGINIA in 1924 when I was an ensign. Prior to his arrival Rochefort had told me that "he had private information from a friend in Washington that a special agent from a certain naval officer on Admiral King's staff was coming out to investigate you and me."

Q: Not a Chief Yeoman.

Layton: This is right. Rochefort said that he'd come to Pearl Harbor under the guise of setting up facilities for your Intelligence Center; to look into the requirements, to see what kind of desks and chairs and what they'll have to furnish you etc. He said, "If I were you, I'd be very cagey with this fellow." And I said, "I will be."

He said, "It may be they don't like the way we work so close together. Maybe you had better pretend that you and I don't get along so well."

I said, "Joe, if that's the way you want it, I'll do it. Whatever you say."

Q: That's sad, isn't it?

Layton: And he said, "All right. Let's play it real carefully and if they ask you about me, you say, 'Oh, yes, we get along officially but we're not real personal friends.'"

I said, "You want it that way?"

He said, "Yes." So when this yeoman came to see me, I

remembered him as the mail orderly on the WEST VIRGINIA. After some talk he asked me my relations with Rochefort and I gave the "agreed reply." He merely grunted and said that Rochefort had said about the same thing concerning me. The rest of our talk dealt with equipment and personnel requirements for the Intelligence Center, and the assurances by him that they would be forthcoming.

He went back and reported -- I've been told -- that Joe and I were not friendly, that we didn't get along well. Now, this could be it. But that couldn't be the truereason -- it could be used as an excuse. I believe the real reason was they didn't want Rochefort there making them appear to be the fools that they were over this "AF" matter, again in the future.

Q: Isn't that tragic?!

Layton: It's disturbing. When you've gone through it and you've seen a man like Rochefort be absolutely speared like a frog and hung out just to dry throughout the rest of the war, when he could have done so much. He did do a lot, even back there. It took years to get him out of "purgatory." But he didn't get his D.S.M.

Q: And he never had Admiral.

Layton: No. Let's change the subject.

Q: Ok. We'll change the subject because we still have some of the war to cover.

Q: Do you think that Admiral Ghormley was mistreated?

Layton: That's a difficult question for me to answer. It was believed that he was not as dynamic and effective a leader as he should have been. Well, of course, there's a lot to be said on his side; communications were very, very bad; he couldn't get messages through, and other difficulties.

On the other hand, Nimitz' decision to appoint Halsey as the commander of that area was a very popular decision. It was received by all the troops with "whoopees" and joy and raised the morale of both the Marines on Guadalcanal and the naval forces down there.

Halsey's appointment may have had some pyschological aspects but this was what we needed at that time; Halsey is remembered as ordering: "Kill Japs, Kill Japs, and kill more Japs."

Q: He was a great leader.

Layton: He was a great leader and he inspired our forces in the South Pacific; it was what we needed at that time. Thereafter, as you know, our operations showed a lot more aggressiveness.

Q: We did talk about the Marshalls and you indicated that the decision was to go to Kwajalein but I think you stopped there. Should we go back and pick up the intelligence at that point.

Layton: Until I had reported to Admiral Nimitz this new situation of continual reinforcement of the perimeter islands of the Marshalls at the expense of Kwajalein atoll, it was rather well understood, but not decided, that our point of attack in the Marshalls would be two of the strongest islands there, ones which would provide us with the best air bases; the Japs had established air bases on atolls at Wotje and Mili and Taroa (Maloelap). Jaluit had good anchorage but didn't have an airfield; it had a sea plane base but was also too far to the south. All preliminary planning considerations had involved outer perimeter islands.

Then, after our successful assault on TARAWA and the Gilberts, we began to see the Japs moving reinforcements from the Kwajalein Headquarters area out to the perimeter islands. Our submarines were busy and effective on the Japanese sea lines of communications from the Empire to the Marshalls. We saw not only army forces and their artillery, but also more air units moving to the perimeter islands along with more equipment. As this Japanese re-deployment picture became clearer, Nimitz asked me to draw up a new order of battle setting forth the new strengths, naval, army, air and construction workers assigned to each of the island groups of the Marshalls. Of course, we had kept this on a day to day basis cross-checked by the latest "available" ration reports and reports of sick days and hospitalized personnel. Then Admiral Nimitz scheduled a conference with his Marshall Islands assault commanders: General "Howling Mad" Smith, Admiral Spruance, Admiral Turner and several others along with their Chiefs of Staff and other staff personnel who had been working on their plans for the assault and capture of selected positions in the Marshalls. Just before this conference with his Task Force commanders, I reviewed with Admiral Nimitz the Marshalls order of battle again; he told me to attend that meeting, along with my intelligence summary and order of battle figures, and be prepared to answer any questions concerning these matters. At the conference, he reviewed this intelligence for them, without saying how he knew the details. He stressed that there was clear evidence of this recent reinforcement of the outer islands at the expense of Kwajalein. He then asked his Task Force Commanders if they still wanted to go where they had been planning to assault. To his Task Force Commanders, there seemed to be only the question of taking two of three selected objectives: Mili, Taroa, or Wotje -- some wanted to take Mili and Taroa, some preferred Wotje and Taroa, while some favored taking Taroa and Mili. Kwajalein was not mentioned by any of them. Nimitz heard all their discussion and preferences with patience; he then said, "No, gentlemen, we are not going there. We're going into Kwajalein."

They all looked at him as if he had lost his mind. They then argued that they had their plans all drawn up, even the details of landing areas, of troop employment and resupply. They wanted to proceed with the plans that they had drawn up after many conferences and discussions together.

Admiral Nimitz said, "I don't care what you've done. Just go back and re-do it and do it for Kwajalein. That's the enemy's weakest point, and is the position where they won't expect us. The Task Force Commanders argued that Japanese air strength deployed to all their strong points would make such a penetration into the central position of Kwajalein too hazardous. They felt that it would be more prudent to assault outer perimeter islands, for which their plans were made, and practically complete. It seemed to me that they had made up their minds and they didn't want to change, despite the "solid" intelligence against such plans.

Admiral Sherman was either the Chief of Staff or the Head of War Plans at that time and, of course, he had had all this intelligence as it developed and was alert to the significance. He then said; "Don't you worry about their air. Our carriers will take care of their air strengths and I think you will all be able to land without major air interference. We're going to have ten new carriers there." He says, "This is going to be a new era in carrier aviation; to have that many to operate to knock down enemy air opposition. I have no doubts, and I think everything will work out fine."

Then they got in this shore bombardment discussion again -- at Tarawa there wasn't enough, so now we had to plan for more. Nimitz said, "Yes, there will be a strong bombardment. We'll knock out the air, so you can go in and bombard their shore defenses at any range you want to."

Well, the astonishment of these senior admirals and one general, his Chief of Staff -- I think it was General Erskine -- was very pronounced. They said, again, they wanted to assault Taroa and Wotje. The Admiral said, "No, gentlemen. I have decided we are going to Kwajalein. The Japanese aren't going to know this, and they're going to be as surprised as you gentlemen are."

Q: He was a real tough character, wasn't he?

Layton: In a nice way. His eyes would sparkle. He would say it just like he had won a bridge hand by clever finesses. It was just marvelous and he would smile his beatific way and say, "No, gentlemen, we're going to Kwajalein."

Q: And he did all of this on this basis of intelligence.

Layton: Well, his decision was based on intelligence plus his preception that the enemy wouldn't be expecting an assault on Kwajalein; knowing the enemy was expecting attacks on the outer perimeter strong points, he saw to it they continued to be deluded in this by ordering continued close reconnaissance of those atolls along with Kwajalein and other atolls. The Task Force Commanders asked what we'd do about Wotje, Taroa, etc., He said, "We'll just let them wither on the vine." Those were his words: "We'll let them wither on the vine."

They looked at him and I think it was a third time that

Howling Mad Smith said, "I think we should go the other way." Admiral Nimitz said, "If you gentlemen don't want to go the way I want you to, I can always get people that will.". . or something like that. I heard that he told Spruance and Smith, (I think it was -- later in his office, when they came back again to argue their points of view) that he told them of his decision and he'd give them three minutes to make up their mind to go his way, or he'd appoint new Task Force Commanders who would do so.

Q: So?

Layton: Yes. This is what I hear from Potter who had this from Nimitz himself. Now I wasn't in the cabin at that time. Potter wanted to know if I was and I said, "No." But I heard Nimitz tell them that if they didn't want to go the way he wanted them to go, he'd get commanders that would.

Q: Well, I'm sure you have to use that tactic if people are being obstructive.

Layton: He wanted to point out to them that they were talking to their Commander-in-Chief; that he made the decisions and they weren't going to sit around and tell him what he was going to do. This was why he was a great commander. He could do it in a nice way; there is no doubt that they got his "message," loud and clear; there could be no doubt as to who was responsible for the over all direction of the war in the Pacific Ocean Areas!

Q: Which is the final.

Layton: He didn't often have to say that.

Q: No. Only about once!

Layton: That's right. I think that covers that but this was where a recording would have been useful and historic too. Incidentally, about the time we went into Guadalcanal P. V. Mercer (a classmate of mine) reported to the Headquarters to act as Flag Secretary, temporarily. He made the suggestion that we have a tape recorder installed to record all the conferences (and other such official meetings) in Admiral Nimitz's office; all the briefings and official staff conferences etc. The record would be edited by the Admiral and his staff, and kept for historical records. Admiral Nimitz said, "No!"

Mercer started to argue again that it would be good for history and so forth and Nimitz said, "No, didn't you understand me? I said, no." And that ended it!

Q: I would think that was the right decision anyway. For history it would be nice now. But people -- I would have felt his decision right. I'm sure he'd appreciate that anyway.

Do you have any intelligence reports in the Alaskan invasion -- Attu, Kiska?

Layton: That was a typical invasion of an island that we had owned. Like later on the island of Guam. We had owned the island of Guam since 1898, yet -- you won't believe it -- but we didn't have good maps of our own island. The Japanese had better maps of Guam than we had, and they had occupied it only in 1941.

The Japanese had taken Attu in early June 1942 as a feint in the battle of Midway, to draw our attention away. Fortunately, we knew about it, so the feint didn't work.

When the decision was made to assault and recapture Attu, we tried to get some good maps, but found that there were no good terrain maps.

In amphibious warfare, the soldiers on the ground -- Marines or Army, want to know what are the details of the terrain: where can it give the enemy cover? Where can you use it as the best place for getting equipment ashore? Where to put your people ashore? Where to build an airfield, etc.

We didn't have any proper maps of Attu, but Attu being within flying range of our bases in Alaska and the Aleutians, we flew aerial photographic reconnaissance missions from just after their occupation by the Japanese until just before landing our assault troops. Photographic interpretation kept track of the build-up of the enemy's defensive installations and, despite Jap camouflage, produced some accurate terrain maps. We knew the Japanese order of battle rather accurately, so the job was to assault the island and retake them.

By this time it was clear that they were not going to surrender. As a matter of fact, it was contrary to their traditions for anyone to surrender. So they would have to be killed; to the last man

Now back to Attu, it was a straightforward operation. We got our intelligence and our people went ashore and killed the Japs. Kiska was a different thing. We gathered the intelligence, got already to go, and went ashore after a terrific bombardment, and -- were our faces red! There wasn't a Jap there; intelligence had given us no indication that they had left! The only indication we had was one aerial photograph, in which the photo-interpretors noted that "things were strewn around the beaches and other places as if it had been abandoned'." But it was just as well. It saved a lot of lives.

Now there's another thing that should be mentioned, I think, and that's Eniwetok. At the same time that Admiral Nimitz had made his mind up on Kwajalein, we had been observing a big buildup at Eniwetok, (which the Japanese called "Brown") at the same time of the build-up of forces on the perimeter islands of the Marshalls was taking place. Eniwetok was in a very strategic location with respect to Kwajalein and would interfere with what we had in mind as our next strategic mission.

Admiral Nimitz said, "I want you to keep your eye on Eniwetok. I think we will have forces available to go after that place right after Kwajalein but I will clear this with King." He sent messages back to King and the Joint Chiefs of Staff that if it was feasible, he wanted to assault and occupy Eniwetok as soon as he had seized his position in the Marshalls. He would do it with his reserves, if he didn't have to commit them at Kwajalein. That was approved.

When these commanders were told to plan for Eniwetok, they thought he was being too confident. They felt that they would need all of our forces for the assault on the Marshalls; that there would be very severe fighting for Kwajalein. Nimitz was confident that assaulting the enemy's weakened position, Kwajalein, would not require committing his reserve and that therefore he would still have adequate forces to capture Eniwetok.

So they were told to plan as if they had a reserve. Now in this connection I might mention that they did make a sound decision, which they recommended to Nimitz -- that they seize a fleet anchorage in the Marshalls. They didn't want to take all of their forces into Kwajalein lagoon although it is the largest in the world. They wanted to seize Majuro atoll and use its lagoon as an advanced anchorage for the reserve, the supply and logistic vessels and for a refuelling anchorage. Nimitz agreed.

The order of battle for Majuro at that time listed the troop strength as six Japanese. When I read this number at the breifing, General "Howling Mad" Smith said, "You mean six thousand." I said, "No, six." He offered to bet "a quart of the best bourbon whiskey" that the number of Japs on Majuro would turn out to be "nearer 600 Japs than 6" - - - I accepted the bet. When the Marshalls - Eniwetok assaults had been completed and General Smith returned to his Headquarters at Pearl Harbor, he sent his car and driver to pick me up one evening before dinner. Arriving at his Quarters I found his staff assembled. General Smith presented me with a bottle of bourbon, wrapped with ribbons of scarlet and gold, the Marine Corps' colors, remarking that he was glad that the number of Japs on Majuro were so few, adding that my estimate was also wrong -- since there had been only one Jap, instead of the six I had said.

At about that time, intelligence began to show a concentration of the Japanese fleet at Truk. A Marine photographic plane flew out of the Solomons to Truk to make a photographic reconnaissance. Admiral Yamamoto realized that a four-engine Liberator, flying over Truk was probably on a photographic reconnaissance. Our previous photographic reconnaissance flights by "Liberators" over long ranges, such as over Tarawa, over the Marshalls, and over Eniwetok had been followed by our attacks. He decided Truk was no place to keep his fleet, so he ordered them out.

Truk was their main overseas naval base: nearly all their submarine tenders were there, as were their ammunition ships, repair ships, fleet oilers, supply ships as well as battleships, cruisers, destroyers etc. The combatant ships left on Yamamoto's orders, the fleet auxiliaries were delayed for some reason and were sunk by our Carrier Task Force raid in February 1943. This broke the back of the Japanese Navy, broke it as a potential offensive force, by destroying its fleet-train. We sank tremendous numbers of vital auxiliaries, the submarine tenders, repair ships, ammunition ships, supply ships, oil tankers -- the kinds of ships you can't replace. Without these, distant overseas operations are practically impossible.

I talked to some Japanese after I retired in Japan (1959-1963). They don't normally speak about the war, but they wanted to talk about the Truk raid. They emphasized that this is the "one that broke their back." They could "endure" Midway. Yes, they'd lost their carriers, they'd lost their carrier pilots, which were more important than the carriers. But the Truk raid effectively eliminated any thought of offensive, forward operations of their fleet, thereafter.

In my opinion, one of the reasons for the tremendous success of the Truk raid was that the Task Force Commander, Admiral Mitscher, had on board (as did two or three other carrier division commanders) "combat intelligence units," which performed tactical radio intercept operations for their commanders. They gave "early warning" of enemy scouting or search planes up, or of strikes being formed. Awareness of a scout plane approach enabled the commander to vector out his fighters to intercept and shoot down the search plane or scout. If the scout or search plane sighted our forces, his radioed "contact report" was also intercepted, alerting the commander that his forces' presence was known to the enemy. In fact, one factor in the Truk raid's success was that of surprise; we shot down their search and scout planes before they could get off a "contact report," so our strike was an initial, abrupt, surprise to the Japanese.

We were bothered earlier in the war by Jap night aerial torpedo attacks on ships. We lost the CHICAGO this way. The Japanese would come up on either bow of a formation in what they call an "anvil attack" -- attack units spread about ninety degrees, one to the other, -- and attack from both bows with torpedoes, after other planes, float planes etc. had dropped flares and lighted floats in line with the formation. The attackers could see their angle of attack by the float-lights while our ships were illuminated by the parachute flares, which lit up the area almost as if it were daylight.

Admiral Radford devised a method to use his radio-intercept unit ("combat intelligence unit") which had been assigned him to nullify that night aerial torpedo attack. The officer in charge of the unit would keep Admiral Radford completely aware of the attack commander's orders so that Radford could maneuver his Task Force to evade and frustrate those night aerial torpedo attacks. For example, when the attacking groups were ordered to form up on either bow of the Task Force, preparatory to the attack, Radford would radio his force to stand by for an increase of speed to 28 knots and an emergency turn of from 135° to 180° from their previous course. When the enemy groups were reported in position and the float planes had begun to drop flares and float lights, Radford would execute his speed and turn signals. The enemy attack planes on approaching their "release-torpedoes" position would sight their targets on almost a reverse course, high-tailing it at a speed almost equal to their torpedoes speed. The attack commander would then cancel the attack and order his group to reform ahead of Radford's force. When they had reformed and the order given for flares and float-lights to be dropped, Radford would repeat his high-speed, simultaneous reverse, and the attacking group would again be frustrated. After several attempts, cancelled due to Radford's high speed reverses, the attack commander would order his units to close and attack when their supply of flares or float lights or gasoline became low. Since the ships' speeds were only slightly less than torpedo speeds, the ships had opportunity to avoid the torpedoes, paralleling their tracks. Moreover, Radford's maneuvers spoiled the Japanese "anvil attack" of having their own torpedoes criss-cross the Task Force track, since by reversing the course it forestalled the "criss-cross" of enemy torpedoes. This is, in my opinion, a good example of a practical use of instantaneous tactical intelligence. It's success spelled the end of a severe Japanese threat to our control of the sea in the Pacific.

Now the Japanese, in their own official reports, have said that they had radio intelligence units on certain of their flagships, and the commander was authorized to use the tactical intelligence gained by their radio intelligence unit against the enemy. They used it in Java Sea; the Japanese had Dutch and English speaking radio intelligence officers with the Commander down there and he knew when our ships were voice signals to one another, what they were going to do, and was enabled to take counter-action thereto.

Q: It is so simple as you explain it, that you can't imagine anyone daring to go to sea without having it and then using it.

Layton: Of course, the number of people you could have were limited in number. The man had to be perfectly and linguistically qualified because this language isn't what the Japanese use every day. The specially trained radio intercept operators that were used were the "old hands" with the most experience, and there was always a critical shortage of these highly skilled and specially trained personnel.

Q: I wanted to know if there was something about the Marianas, Philippines or submarine campaigns that we should cover.

Layton: Well, the Marianas was again -- intelligence-wise we did not have accurate maps and charts and stuff. The Marianas were beyond the range of our reconnaissance aircraft, so a carrier task force, under Mitscher, went up to make a sweep of the Marianas but primarily to fly aerial photo missions. Our attack surprised the Japanese; they didn't ever believe that our carrier task force would go that far. The aerial photo reconnaissance was for the planning-planning for the future invasion of the Marianas - Saipan, Tinian and Guam.

Just before the invasion of the Marianas, we knew that the Japanese had a new "defense plan for the Empire." We knew that the old plan had included the Marshalls in a list of areas "critical to the defense of the Empire." When we attacked Kwajalein and Eniwetok, the Japanese fleet did not assemble and come to those areas to contest control of the seas with us. They just had a whipping down in the Solomons, and didn't have sufficient naval air left. They had tried their night aerial torpedo attacks to drive us from the Marshalls and Gilberts when we assaulted Tarawa, but were foiled by the Radford maneuvers I've described.

Just before the Marianas campaign opened, we received a copy of an old Japanese Defense Plan which we now knew had been superseded. The Marshalls had been removed from the old plan, as we suspected, but the Marianas, the Philippines, the Aleutians, the Carolines, Taiwan and Okinawa remained as "vital areas to the defense of the Empire"; places where major assaults/invasions by U. S. forces would be counter attacked by all available Japanese strengths, naval, air and ground. It was very valuable to get this document, this basic strategical defense plan even though superceded. We sent it out to the Fleet with a covering letter signed by the Chief of Staff, Admiral McMorris stating that a new plan was in effect, superceding this one but we believed that the basic strategic principles of this old plan were still applicable to our forth-coming assault on the Marianas.

Q: How did you get it?

Layton: Well, I have to go back now; In support of the landing in Hollandia of General MacArthur, the Carrier Task Force first struck Palau (in the Western Carolinas); they gave Palau a real "going-over." By this time, Admiral Yamamoto being dead, Admiral Koga had taken over. The night following the strike by our carrier-Task Force, he and his staff left Palau in two flying boats to fly to the Philippines. Admiral Koga's Chief of Staff was in plane number two. Plane number one and Koga were never heard from again.

The chief of staff's plane ran into a terrific storm and

was forced to land on the water and was wrecked in the Philippines, near Cebu, I believe. There were guerrillas there who captured the Chief of Staff and his brief case. The guerrillas sent word to MacArthur's headquarters that they had captured a briefcase containing important papers. MacArthur's headquarters had the Seventh Fleet send one of its submarines to get the documents. At MacArthur's headquarters "Nisei" translaters did a sloppy, non-naval translation of the document in question and sent a dispatch to Washington and Nimitz outlining the gist of it. I suggested to Admiral Nimitz that he request a photostatic copy of the document by air. He agreed and the message was sent and a photostat copy was received by us in a very short time. We translated it that night and ran off many copies on the mimeograph and prepared a covering letter sending it to all unit commanders of the Marianas Invasion forces, then assembled in Eniwetok. Admiral Nimitz authorized a four-engine flying boat to carry this letter and translation with other last minute official mail to Eniwetok. Nimitz wanted to get it in the hands of every Task Force and Task Unit commander before they sailed for the assault on the Marianas. Of course, foremost in our minds was to get it in Spruance's hands and into Mitscher's hands so they would read it and study it.

In this plan it said, "if the enemy attacks in the Marianas, we'll concentrate our forces and attack and annihilate him." That's what they tried to do.

If you <u>know</u> the enemy is going to do something, or you're <u>pretty sure</u> he's going to do something, you have an advantage.

I believe that this plan was one of the reasons Spruance took a cautious and prudent attitude when he received further intelligence, after the invasion of Saipan had commenced, that the Japanese navy was concentrating. He realized that if he went running after the Japanese fleet, Jap aircraft could bomb him from Guam, Tinian, Saipan, or Rota, or other bases, land on the carriers to the west of him, refuel/reload and come back and attack his forces again. While planes from the carriers would attack him, then rearm and refuel at the Marianas bases, and bomb his forces while returning to their carriers. A true shuttle bombing! Also, planes would come from the Empire through Iwo Jima, refuel and strike his force, then land on Guam, Rota, Tinian or Saipan and refuel and rearm and attack again. He was smart enough to realize these options open to the enemy, and to stay close to the invasion area, which he had been instructed to defend, while he "clobbered" the enemy airfields in that area so they can't be used for such shuttle bombing. That became the famous "Marianas Turkey Shoot..." the Japanese were never so surprised in their life...they couldn't get over the fact that they sent over some 275 planes to attack Spruance and Mitscher and only some 35, or thereabouts, came back.

Q: That's incredible really. Except this was proper planning.

Layton: Yes, But now, I'd like to go back to the Invasion of Kwajalein and relate a true story of the Japanese Secret Charts of the Mandated Islands. Sometimes, things turn out to be fortuititous. At the time of the invasion of Kwajalein, a small army raider type unit was to seize two small islands astride the south-eastern entrance to Kwajalein lagoon just before the assault was to commence. Both of these units landed on the wrong island, each one island too far to the west. The western most unit immediately encountered some Japanese naval personnel, whose ship had been sunk in the preliminary bombardment and bombing. The senior officer of these Japanese was carrying a roll of charts, all edged in red, which were seized. Our standard instructions identified documents edged in red as Japanese top secret - so the U.S. officer in charge got word to Admiral Turner of these red bordered charts; Turner had them picked up and taken aboard his flagship, where they were identified as the top secret charts of the Mandated Islands, showing areas that were mined and areas that had been cleared of coral heads and wire-dragged to a certain depth. Copies of the Kwajalein chart were immediately reproduced on Turner's flagship and furnished all commands, and all ships. That chart was used to clear Kwajalein atoll of mines and to guide the Amphibious Forces to safe, sheltered anchorages within the lagoon. These charts were later used for Eniwetok, Saipan, Tinian, Ulithi, etc. etc. Sometimes you wonder if the unit that landed on the wrong island didn't have some divine guidance.

Another incident that had to do with intelligence happened on Attu. In all these invasions we had instructions out to all forces on how to handle captured documents and prisoners; our units from the Joint Intelligence Center Pacific Ocean Area were attached to each amphibious assault to examine the prisoners and documents for immediate tactical intelligence of value. Instructions stressed that captured documents were often of vital importance, showing troop concentration, artillery locations and other important matters -- that troops were not to pocket them or keep them for souvenirs but, instead, turn them in for examination by Intelligence. The instructions also said that troops turning in captured documents would receive a worthless one after the assault was completed. At Attu, an army unit captured some documents but instead of turning these in, as required by their instructions, these soldiers put them in their pockets. As they advanced they were taken under mortar fire, and one of the men had his leg blown off. Medics took him on a stretcher to the dressing station. As his wound was being dressed there, the Medic found this Japanese document in his pocket. Examined by intelligence, it proved to be a sketch showing the location of the Japanese artillery and the mortars. So, had he followed the instructions and turned that document in, the chances are that those artillery and mortar positions would have been taken under counter-battery fire and he wouldn't have lost his leg. This was another lesson in intelligence.

Q: I'm sure it was effective.

Layton: You've asked about submarine intelligence. In the early part of the war before Captain Holmes was made a part of Captain Rochefort's organization, it was my duty to inform Commander

Submarines (our headquarters were then at the Submarine Base, Pearl Harbor) of important Japanese shipping movements as obtained from radio intelligence. He, in turn, could tell his submarines. The submarines had a little code to use in messages to their submarines: something like - "Bears" stood for cruisers, "Bulls" represented destroyers, and "Whales" was the word for carriers, etc.: Commander Submarines could tell a submarine: "you might find a bear in your patrol area E-6," or some such. This was done in case the Japanese were able to break this message, they would not learn the source of our information, not knowing what a bear or area E-6 was.

They had some great successes. In one case, for example, a submarine skipper reported that he had sank a large vessel, possibly a tanker of about 6,000 tons at night, off Tokyo Bay. Radio intelligence had picked up a distress message sent by the MIZUHO a big seaplane carrier reporting that she was attacked, and was sinking.

So when this submarine skipper made his oral report to Commander Submarines, he was told that his victim was the MIZUHO, of around 14,000 tons, instead of a "tanker of about 6,000 tons." His official Patrol Report then listed his victim as the 14,000 ton seaplane carrier "MIZUHO."

Later, as we developed more and more intelligence on Japanese shipping and convoy routes, Holmes was assigned, through JICPOA, the task of supervising and handling intelligence for our submarines. Being an old submariner, his personal direction and liaison with the staff of ComSubPac was most effective and appreciated. By communications intelligence we also learned that our torpedoes were not exploding as designed. Eventually this evidence caused major investigations into the reasons for our poor torpedo performance. It was discouraging: a submarine would attack his target and his torpedoes fail to explode!

There had been a lot of talk about de-activating the magnetic exploder, it being suspected as being at fault. The Bureau of Ordnance, and the ordnance experts said, "Oh, no, no. The exploder is fine, there must be something wrong with your preparation or firing procedures etc. Finally a submarine reported attacking and sinking two enemy aircraft carriers north of Truk. Radio inteligence, including traffic analysis, however, noted that the two carriers and their escorts arrived safely at Truk and were preparing to return to Japan, after refuelling. I brought these unpleasant facts to Admiral Nimitz's attention; he called for a conference with ComSubPac, Admiral Lockwood, and his staff to discuss measures to be taken to rectify our deficient torpedo performance. After considerable discussion, Admiral Nimitz said, "I think we ought to deactivate the magnetic exploders. Admiral Lockwood said, "I can't order that." Admiral Nimitz said, "I can, and I will." And Admiral Lockwood said, "I would be happy if you would." Thereafter torpedo performance improved but was not fully satisfactory. Admiral Lockwood then had an investigation made into the contact-exploder and found mechanical faults in design, which were corrected. The Bureau of Ordnance also made some tests which proved the torpedoes were running deeper than designed (and deeper than the depths "set" on the torpedo). This was also corrected and torpedo performance, and sinkings of Japanese ships thereafter moved on a rising curve.

Q: I wanted to ask you one final question before we go on to the surrender. Did the fact that you were a lieutenant commander during -- let me ask you first, were you a lieutenant commander during all of this period?

Layton: I didn't keep a record so I don't know the date I made commander, and I don't remember the date that I was promoted to captain.

Q: I see, Did the fact that you were a lieutenant commander during some of this period hamper your relationships?

Layton: No, not at all.

Q: So then you went to Guam.

Layton: So then the Headquarters moved to Guam in January 1945.
In August the Headquarters was to send a representative to Manila; the Japanese were sending some people there for preliminary surrender negotiations. Admiral Sherman was told by Admiral Nimitz to go as his representative. I knew Admiral Sherman was going; he sent one of his people to get some more

information from me which I prepared for him, for this trip to Manila. The next morning -- the morning that Forrest Sherman had departed -- I went in, as usual, at eight o'clock to brief Admiral Nimitz. He said, "What are you doing here?" in a tone I had never heard him use. I said, "Admiral, it's eight o'clock."

He said, "I know. But what are you doing here?"

I said, "I came to brief you, Sir."

He said, "You're supposed to be in Manila."

I said, "Well, no one told me."

He said, "I told Forrest Sherman to take you and he said he would."

And I said, "Well, he didn't say a word to me."

"You mean to say that he didn't give you any word of this at all?"

And I said, "Not one word. Nor did I know that you wanted me to go, or I could have done some preparatory work."

Well, I could see that he was vexed and upset. All I know is that when Forrest Sherman came back, he soon sent for me and I've never seen a more chastened Forrest Sherman in my life. He was generally pretty aggressive and very self-confident, but it was evident to me that he'd just finished listening to Nimitz's censure -- his apology for leaving me behind was sincere. It was an oversight; it just slipped his mind. He said, "I never thought about it again until I returned and Nimitz sent for me; I've never been "read off" like he did. And I want you to know that I'm very sorry."

Q: You were an innocent bystander.

Layton: So then came the time of the surrender. Nimitz sent for me -- we were talking about whether or not there were going to be continued acts of violence against the established government of Japan by dissident military groups. Whether the Japanese military would oppose the surrender -- oppose the Government's will.

I said that I thought that the Japanese people and most of the military would follow the Emperor's will, although a few of the radical military might be against a surrender. Later, when Admiral Nimitz told me he was taking me to the Surrender Ceremonies with him as a reward for my "long and devoted service to him," he again asked me if I thought there'd be any troubles when our forces landed at Yokosuka. I said not in my opinion, but that I hoped he'd take as a Marine orderly, one who was a crack pistol shot, "just in case."

He said, "They won't attack me. They'd attack MacArthur."

I said, "Not the Japanese." MacArthur didn't win this war as far as the Japanese are concerned. It's been your carriers that have been attacking the cities with carrier raids and it's been the B-29s based in your area that carried the bombs to Japan ¢ including the "A" Bombs. . . they know that they have no shipping; they know it's naval power that brought Japan to its knees; you're the one they would kill, not MacArthur, if they were to try such a thing.

He then asked me if I was a good shot with a pistol, since

I would accompany him instead of the Marine orderly, as I'd suggested.

Thereafter we fired .45 Colts on his pistol range to get to re-train my shooting eye until we left/for Tokyo Bay and the surrender.

Layton: I accompanied Admiral Nimitz when he went ashore at Yokosuka, with Admiral Halsey, when we landed the Marines there at the same time that MacArthur and the first troops landed at Atsugi by aircraft. There were no incidents. After the surrender, I suggested to him that he might want to take the afternoon off; that I had already gone (the previous day) to Kamakura and looked it over and was sure it was all right. Kamakura was never bombed, you know; it's an old historic area and a lovely spot. Cryptomeria trees and old shrines. It is the site of the Great Buddha. It was once the military capital of Japan, also the site of the Tsuragaoka-Hachiman shrine, established by the first Shogun, Yoritomo in the twelfth century. Admiral Nimitz said that he'd like too -- that he hadn't been in Kamakura for many years. We did some sightseeing in Kamakura, including the Great Buddha and the shrines. A photographer took pictures of Admiral Nimitz standing at the Hachiman shrine. This shrine, to many Japanese symbolized the God of War. I thought it ironic that their "God of War" was meeting his conqueror, Nimitz!

We went down south along the seaside of the peninsula from there, (I used to live down in this area so I knew it very well, and then returned to Yokosuka).

He told me that evening, "I want to thank you for a very pleasant afternoon. It was one which I would consider appropriate to top off the surrender." He seemed happy to go off and take a trip through the countryside.

Q: And so that pretty well takes care of us up to the end of the war, doesn't it? Now, between the end of the war and your next duty, you were in Washington, during which period the Congressional hearings took place. Do you have anything to add to that?

Layton: No, I don't think so. We covered that before and it's covered in the record pretty well.

Q: Why did you go to your next job which seems such a change from your prior duties, because you went to the U. S. Naval Net Depot at Tiburon?

Layton: Well, this illustrates the fickle character of the Bureau of Personnel and the officer assignment division. Sometime after the surrender, Bupers sent a dispatch to Nimitz saying they were going to detach me and order me to a command afloat, as I had not had such duty since 1940. I was pleased at the prospects of a command at sea. I had requested Admiral Nimitz for sea duty several times during the war but he had always refused saying I was more valuable for the war effort in my current assignment.

Soon Admiral Nimitz was detached, with orders to Washington as Chief of Naval Operations. My orders then came, but not to a ship; they were to Com 12, San Francisco, for sea command, as directed by Bupers. The Joint Congressional Investigation of Pearl Harbor had been ordered, and on reporting at San Francisco I was ordered to Washington for temporary duty with the Judge Advocate General in connection with my appearance before the Joint Congressional Investigation of Pearl Harbor.

After reaching Washington in early December 1945, I was told to "stand by" -- that my appearance before the Investigation was not yet scheduled. I inquired at Bupers as to what command I would get. Their reply was they wouldn't know until I was "available," and since my appearance before the Investigation was not yet scheduled, they would have to wait to see what ships were then available. But they did assure me that I would get a command, "a good command," as soon as available.

It was late February 1946 before I was finally called to testify at the Hearings. When I had been "released" from the Investigation and made "available for orders," I again contacted Officer Detail in Bupers. The same person (an old shipmate and friend) now said that due to the "roll-up" (then nearing completion) and "moth-balling" of much of the fleet, Bupers didn't have any ships available to which they could order me. It was suggested that since this situation would continue for some time, I should chose a shore-billet that I wanted and "hide for a while" -- that after the long war time separation from my family, I deserved a "breathing spell." I found out that the

Naval Net Depot Tiburon was included in the post-war organization, with a Captain's billet in command, so I requested it and received orders there, promptly.

During the next two years I inquired of Bupers concerning my promised "command at sea" and was told that I'd receive orders in the Spring of 1947 to a A.G.C. (Amphibious Command Ship). As that time neared, the number of ships available for command became less with the reduction in the size of the navy. When Spring of 1947 arrived, without any orders as yet, I inquired of Bupers again, and was told that with fewer ships, commands were difficult to schedule, but that I would receive orders "in the near future." At this time an old friend (who had just left Bupers) told me that I would be given "excuses," by Bupers, but "no command."

Prior to this, on a brief visit to Buord in Washington (the Net Depot's Bureau) I had called on Admiral Nimitz (C.N.O.). He recommended that I apply for Special Duty (Intelligence) as soon as the legislation, authorizing Special Duty categories (in Intelligence, Communications, Law, Hydrography, Public Relations, etc.) was passed by the Congress. He said that my value to the navy would be enhanced and that my particular duties over the years, having been in intelligence, made such a choice appropriate and fitting. As I knew Admiral Nimitz was strongly supporting that legislation, the "1947 Personnel Act," as was Bupers, I began to study that piece of legislation. About that time, the Office of Naval Intelligence, in personal letters to me, began to urge me to apply for Special Duty (Intelligence).

I applied for it and was accepted for that category in mid 1948. I was then ordered to command the new Naval Intelligence School, then being established at the Naval Receiving Station, Washington, D. C.

As the Deputy Director of ONI expressed it: "we have problems." We've got a new intelligence school (Admiral Nimitz backed it one hundred percent) which has language training along with it, several languages. We're going to have professional intelligence officers from now on. In time, it will eliminate the problems we have had -- personnel not properly trained for intelligence duties. It will help, to have these trained people to fill Intelligence billets afloat and ashore. Eventually, commanders and senior officers of the future will have an understanding of the need for intelligence, or with personal intelligence experience; it will be the greatest thing for our Navy that ever happened. We want you to go over and run that school. We couldn't think of anybody that knows more about it and who can teach it, for this purpose. The Army has had an intelligence school for their kind, field intelligence, but our school will aim at the broadest field; we want you to take this."

I said, "Fine. I'll do it."

Well, that was it. It was very rewarding. I thought it was a very fine thing; the people were wonderful -- of those graduated in June 1950, four went out to the Far East area, where we served together under ComNavFE.

After I had been Director of the Naval Intelligence School for almost two years, I wanted to go to Com 14 as District

Intelligence Officer. I had never been a Distric Intelligence Officer -- Vice Admiral McMorris was Com 14 and in a little personal note said he'd like to have me come out there on his staff. My former Assistant in Fleet Intelligence during the war was District Intelligence Officer but he was ill with multiple sclerosis. The doctors had suggested that since this officer had been there a long time with deteriorating health, perhaps a change might be beneficial; arrangements with ONI were being made so that he could go to New Orleans. ONI told me the same thing, and that they would agree to me going to Honolulu and D.I.O. 14 N.D. So my orders were cut to go to Pearl Harbor as a District Intelligence Officer. I arrived there in late June just as the shooting started in Korea. Subsequently ONI ordered me to "take the first plane" and go to Commander Naval Forces, Far East and report for temporary duty to Admiral Joy, as Intelligence Officer.

Arriving at ComNavFE's Headquarters in Tokyo at two o'clock in the morning, I found the four new graduates from Naval Intelligence School at work preparing the material for the intelligence annex of the ComNavFE's Operation Plan. Those lads worked all day and all night for three or four days to put together the intelligence annex, an exercise they had gone through at the Intelligence School on their last school "problem," so they knew how and why. We received many compliments on it. ComNavFE's original staff was small and not organized for a shooting war. After some delays, an Intelligence Section of 30 personnel spaces was approved; but no additional intelligence officers reported for several months. After Inchon landings, when our objectives were secured and everything looked good, I was finally released from the "temporary additional duty" and returned to Pearl Harbor. For more than two months I had urged ONI to order a regular relief for me so I could return to my regular assignment. That whole tour embittered me: ONI could rush me out there along with the four newly graduated intelligence officers (whom they got from various places) plus two of my assistants in Pearl Harbor (also graduates of the Naval Intelligence School). Despite repeated requests, ONI apparently could not provide replacements for those officers, or for myself; All had been suddenly sent out on "temporary additional duty" orders. ONI's excuse was that when the Reserves were called, they had a 30-day waiting period before reporting, and many were given extensions for "sickness," or "family illness," or other reasons. That, plus bureaucratic bungling and bureaucratic indifference were the causes for the delays in receiving the officer personnel necessary to do the job. After these facts were brought to the attention of the Director of Naval Intelligence, changes were made in personnel policies. I returned to Pearl Harbor in late October/early November 1950 and had just about caught up on deferred work in my office, when on 2 or 3 January 1951, I received dispatch orders to report immediately to CINCPAC/CINCPAC Fleet as Assistant Chief of Staff - Intelligence. Admiral Radford was CINCPAC/CINCPAC Fleet.

Q: So now you are over at Admiral Radford's headquarters, back again at CinCPac Fleet, right?

Layton: And CinCPac. The only thing that I think of particular interest then was that there was, by direction of Washington, a tripartite conference in Singapore between representatives of CinCPac, the Commander-in-Chief of Far Eastern station (the British Commander-in-Chief of all three services in the Far East with headquarters in Singapore), and the French Commander-in-Chief in the Far East, Marshal Delatte d'Tassigne. One of the results of this conference was an agreement that there be an Intelligence Conference by the representatives of those three commands to exchange and discuss intelligence on the situation in the Far East every six months. One of the reasons for this was the rise and spread of Communism in the Far East, as seen in the Viet Minh fighting the French in Indo-China and the HUKS conducting guerrila warfare in the Philippines. The Viet Minh attacks against the French in Indo-China were going on at the same time as our fighting in Korea, and accurate, factual intelligence confirmed Communist aims to control all of French Indo-China, and then all of S.E. Asia thereafter.

CNO told Admiral Radford that the U. S. would participate in these Intelligence Conferences that he should furnish the United States representative. He named me the Senior U. S. Representative and I made arrangements for the U. S. Military, Air and Naval Attaches assigned to S. E. Asia (Thailand, Singapore, Indo-China, Hong Kong and Burma) be invited to attend as part of the U. S. Delegation. CNO added representatives from G-2

War Department, A-2 Air Force, ONI and the Joint Intelligence Group, J.C.S. CinCPac also invited representatives from Commander-in-Chief, Far East -- MacArthur's command.

The first of these meeting was held in Saigon; it was also to establish the organization and the measures, for carrying out our directives, which came from each Nations' Joint Chiefs of Staff. I was carefully instructed that I was authorized to speak, as far as intelligence in the Pacific was concerned, for the Commander-in-Chief and as such, for the United States, as well.

The next Intelligence Conference was in Singapore. At this time, the British recommended that the Australians and New Zealanders officially join as "Observers."

We made good progress: the French would brief us what was going on in Indo-China; the British would cover the Guerilla/Bandit activity in Malaya; we would cover the HUK activity in the Philippines, and a sub-committee would summarise the "high points" of the intelligence developed. More important, in my opinion, than the formal record of these Tri Partite Intelligence Conferences was the personal contacts of the various delegations. The intelligence on current operational matters was valuable and mutual understanding encouraged better exchanges of intelligence on Communist operations and aims in S.E. Asia.

The next meeting was again held in Saigon. On its conclusion, I pointed out to Admiral Radford it was the U. S. turn now; I recommended we invite the participants to come to Pearl Harbor. The problem was distance, of course, and cost of transportation. Admiral Radford put this problem up to CNO, who approved the use of one of the Navy Fleet Logistic Wing aircraft to bring the delegations of the British and the French from Sangley Point (in the Philippines) to Pearl Harbor free of charge and return them to Sangley Point. Unfortunately, although they had accepted and plans laid accordingly, at the last minute the Navy said we could not use the plane as "something unforseen had happened" -- which resulted in CinCPac being forced to withdraw its offer of free transportation from Sangley Point and return.

The French were naturally a little miffed; they had to come, (because we had no airplane to offer them) via Pan American, at considerable expense. The British, on the other hand, came in a British logistic type airplane. Both felt that we had let them down. Admiral Radford knew this, but there was nothing he could do about it although he had protested very strongly.

At the time of our Conference at Pearl Harbor SEATO was in the process of being set-up. We were advised by CNO that we should move at this meeting that since there had been mutual agreements by the British, French, Australian and New Zealand and United States governments, to participate in SEATO, that any further intelligence conferences of this nature, including exchanges of intelligence on S.E. Asia, should be done under the auspices of SEATO. The motion was adopted and that was the last "Tri-Partite Intelligence Conference for South East Asia."

Q: You spoke of Dien Bien Phu.

Layton #2 - 179

Layton: In Singapore, General Cognye (the Head of the French Delegation) brought me a message from his commanding general inviting me "and my party" to come to Hanoi and take a trip in the field with the French forces operating against the Viet Minh, in view of our interest in guerrilla warfare, and in the tactics and types of operations used there.

I sent an outline of this to Admiral Radford saying that I wanted to divert my return to join the French in these field operations in the Hanoi area for about three days, and requested his approval. With his approval, I notified General Cogny of our acceptance and when the Singapore conference was over, I took another Navy Captain, and Army officer, two Marine officers and an Air Force officer with me to Hanoi via Saigon. The Commanding General of French Forces in Indo-China invited us to dinner, and command briefing, after we made our official call on him. He said General Cogny's "2nd Division of March of Tonkin" would start clearing operations the next day early, and that we could join him at his command post then. The French drove us down there early the next day. After reporting to General Cogny, we attended his "command briefing" on the operation which was then in progress. We were each assigned to a combat team. I remained with General Cogny, and travelled with him as he inspected his units and their operations. About 75% of the combat troops were French Legionaires, (which included three U. S. citizens) of which about 75% were German -- many formerly of Hitler's army -- but good, professional soldiers.

All supplies (food, water, ammo, etc.) were air dropped.

Layton #2 - 180

Also, cold beer was dropped for the troops, as well as their regulation wine issue with meals. The water is all polluted. There are no facilities to boil water on such operations.

Q: And your assignments for the rest of your career all are with intelligence, aren't they?

Layton: Yes, as an intelligence specialist, S.D.O. (1630).

Q: And so you went back to be Assistant Director of the Joint Staff for Intelligence and then . . .

Layton: Earlier, I had orders to Rio de Janeiro as Naval Attache. Rio de Janeiro was not my choice, but and if that's where ONI wanted me to go, that was fine with me.

Then orders came which I was very happy to receive -- cancelling my orders to Rio, and ordering me as Naval Attache, Rome. I had just read the dispatch orders when Admiral Radford sent for me. He said, "Well, you're not going to Rio, and you're not going to Rome; I'm going to take you back to Joint Chiefs of Staff." He said, "What the Joint Chiefs of Staff needs is better intelligence appraisals and some intelligence expertise and since I'm going back there as Chairman of the Joint Chiefs of Staff, I'm going to take you back there with me."

Washington was the last place I wanted to go <u>then</u>, but that's where I went.

Later he said, "I don't think you'll regret it. I understand it's going to be the Navy's turn to furnish the senior officer in the Joint Intelligence Group, and the Navy should have a flag officer with intelligence experience to head it. It's headed by an Air Force General now, and before him an Army General, so now it's the Navy's turn. I want you to be there, ready to take that job; I'll see what can be done to have you made a flag officer. Until that time the precept of the Flag Officer Selection Board had not included any S.D.O. Intelligence space.

The Flag Selection Board met that June. When I reported for duty in Washington (30th of June, I think) with the Joint Chiefs of Staff, the Selection Board report came out, and I was happy to find myself on that selection list. That was 1953. I made my number on the 1st of January 1954.

Admiral Radford, being the Chairman of the Joint Staff considered me his personal intelligence officer; he would send down various intelligence requirements, and we would produce the reports required. We would call on each of the three services for their intelligence in response to the problem and we'd put the answers together into a joint estimate. When it went before the Joint Chiefs of Staff, they would ask if it were an agreed estimate. In other words, we didn't give a one-service estimate; we had to have an agreed paper, covering the different views of the services, which sometimes had advantages.

Q: Did you feel a sense of accomplishment, having become a rear admiral?

Layton: I was so busy with our work in the Joint Intelligence Group that I never had time to think in terms of accomplishment.

The Deputy Director for Intelligence of the Joint Staff was a full member of the Intelligence Advisory Committee, the nation's highest intelligence committee, and advisory to the National Security Council. He is also a member, and Chairman of the Joint Intelligence Committee of the Joint Chiefs of Staff. The C.I.A. is the permanent Chairman of the Intelligence Advisory Committee.

Q: That's interesting.

Layton: If the subject is non-controversial, all goes along very smoothly. But if the subject of the estimate bears on some aspect of our policy, the proceedings become more complicated due to the Central Intelligence Agency's participation in these things; very often the CIA wanted to use an intelligence estimate of the IAC to change our national policy. Hence, the estimate sought by the CIA was often "slanted," or emphasized toward a policy desired by the CIA. This is in clear conflict with the intelligence axiom that the intelligence estimate, on which policy will be based, must be honest, objective and without bias.

Q: Do you have a for instance of that?

Layton: I have many but I don't want to right now. It would take you too long.

Q: Could you not give me one?

Layton: Yes, I can give you one example. There was an agreed estimate of the capacity of the Trans-Siberian Railroad -- its tons per day capacity. For many years the IAC had agreed that the capacity of the Trans-Siberian Railway to the Far East was, let us say, 1000 tons a day. I don't remember the exact figure -- let us take that figure as an example.

When I was on Admiral Radford's staff in 1951-53, this agreed capacity of the Trans-Siberian Railway was raised from 1000 to 1400 tons per day. It's a double-track railroad but runs for thousands of miles through rugged areas and is subject to delays. At the time there had been no reports on increased siding's or freight handling yards along the railway to indicate increased efficiency or capacity and this sudden change, without any intelligence to indicate a "why" was puzzling. About that time Admiral Radford was going to Washington to confer with the J.C.S. and C.N.O.; he took me along to look into this matter. We knew that sometime previously Admiral Sherman, the CNO, had proposed to the Joint Chiefs of Staff, placing a naval blockade along the China coast; this proposal went from the J.C.S. to the Secretary of Defense, who put it before the National Security Council. This measure had been proposed after the Communist Chinese entry into the Korean War, and at a time when they were being very hellicose. The N.S.C. asked the I.A.C. for an up-to-date estimate of the capacity of the Trans-Siberian Railway -- and came up with the new estimate of increased capacity. The proposed blockade, was turned down by the National Security Council; their reasoning was based on the premise that a naval blockade would not be effective since the Trans-Siberian Railroad could carry all the cargo necessary to supply the Chinese. The National Security Council's action, or decision, was based on a "slanted," a biased or false estimate of the Trans-Siberian Railway's capacity. Admiral Radford and I were curious as to why, and how, the suddenly increased carrying capacity of that railway came about. In Washington, I went to the Army, who were the experts in railroad intelligence and asked why this capacity went from 1000 tons to 1,400 tons? The Director of Military Intelligence, the G-2 of the Army (whom I knew personally) said that he didn't know, but he would find out for me. We went to the section in G-2 that handled railways, their equipment, carrying capacities etc, to get theanswer at first hand. Enroute to that area, I told General Partridge (the G-2 of the Army) the reasons for Admiral Radford's (and my) interest in the suddenly increased estimate of the capacity of the Trans-Siberian Railway. When we arrived at the section of G-2 that handled railway intelligence, we found that the officer occupying the desk was a British exchange officer from the Royal Engineers; a British Army officer in charge of the U. S. Army's G-2 section on railways intelligence! The British government recognized Communist China and were opposed to any naval blockade of China by the U. S., even though British Commonwealth forces were hurt by China's sudden intervention into the Korean War. They didn't want any hinderance to British trade with China!

After about fifteen minutes of investigation, we learned from this British officer that the increase in tonnage capacity per day of the Trans-Siberian Railway had originated in the Joint Intelligence Committee of London.

Q: Of London.

Layton: The British Joint Intelligence Committee of London had previously agreed to this new capacity. They passed it on to the C.I.A. When this matter came up before the U. S. Intelligence Advisory Committee, the U. S. Army used this new figure in its G-2 estimate without seeking the raw intelligence on which it was supposed to be based. The CIA also endorsed the new figure, so that the other members of the IAC then accepted it, without question. This was not the first, nor was it an isolated instance, where the British Intelligence and the U. S. Central Intelligence Agency worked "hand-in-hand" together. Here, the CIA used this intelligence to "shape" and "slant" an intelligence estimate in order to formulate, or influence, a U. S. policy.

Q: Isn't that frightening?

Layton: Now, let me continue. At CinCPac Fleet Headquarters they knew that Washington was saying that "no strategic goods were being trans-shipped from Hong Kong into Communist China." All Hong Kong was doing was being an "entrepôt," receiving from Communist China such materials as pig hides, pig bristles, tung oil and food for Hong Kong but sending no strategic materials to Communist China. That all shipping from Hong Kong to Communist Chinese ports (mostly under the British flag) was sailing "in ballast" -- no cargo, in other words.

From the time of the Korean War and the order to defend Taiwan from Chinese Communist invasion, our aerial surveillance of shipping along the China coast had been intensified. Every navy surveillance and patrol plane carried a camera and photographed each ship sighted from low altitude, recording automatically the time, and also the location, the name and nationality of the ship, its course and speed, etc. We studied and indexed these photographs and compared the results with the consolidated shipping studies we received from Washington. We noted that these reports listed all British flag shipping between Hong Kong and Communist China's ports as being "in ballast," while our photographs of those same ships, on the same voyage, at the same date as listed in the Washington report showed these ships to be fully loaded -- down to their Plimsoll Marks!!

We felt that the CIA's consolidated shipping reports we'd been receiving from Washington (ONI) were, to say the least, inaccurate and misleading. This was another item that I was to take up in Washington when I went back there with Admiral Radford. I brought to Washington a lot of these photographs to show the information we had on specific ships that had been previously listed as "in ballast." Our figures on Hong Kong exports to Communist China, based on our photographs, were four or five times the totals we had received from Washington. First, I found that in Washington the CIA's consolidated shipping report was not questioned by ONI -- it had been accepted without verification. ONI was embarrassed with the data I showed them.

This caused a big hassle when Admiral Radford told Allen Dulles, the Director of the Central Intelligence Agency, that our figures didn't jibe with his, and we could substantiate our data with photographs. Dulles insisted that the CIA's figures were accurate and when Admiral Radford told him of the CIA reports of shipping "in ballast" while our photographs of the named ships, on specific voyages, on listed dates showed those ships loaded down to the Plimsell Marks, Dulles said, "That can't be true, can't be true."

So he sent their Deputy Director for Intelligence, a Mr. Robert Amory to ONI to meet with the Director of ONI and myself on this matter. I went over the previous CIA consolidated shipping reports with Mr. Amory and pulled out about fifty photographs to show the ships listed were loaded, whereas the CIA report listed them in ballast. Amory even said he thought I had faked the photographs. It would seem that his impulse was to accuse me of doing what the CIA does: fake something to prove a point.

The discussions on this subject became quite heated and during these, he let slip the fact that the reports on this British shipping came from British sources, and that the British "official report" stated these ships to be "in ballast," which they, the CIA, "had to accept"; the British wouldn't mislead us," he added. He resented my implication that the British having a different policy regarding Chine, could be expected to mislead

U. S. intelligence concerning their activities in that area involving trade with Communist China.

Q: O my, you're disillusioning me. It is frightening but I presume it is better to know that intelligence can be doctored to prove your point as well as . . .

Layton: Oh, people have known that for years.

Q: Of course, they have.

Layton: It's question of how adept you are at doctoring it. Usually it is the course of action that is adopted as a result of slanted intelligence that causes the difficulties. If the course of action turns out to be a disaster, like the "Bay of Pigs" fiasco, then those responsible run for cover. The Central Intelligence Agency was involved in this fiasco, and the Director of the CIA, Mr. Dulles, the Deputy Director General Cabell, the Deputy Director for Intelligence, Mr. Amory, the Deputy Director for Operations and others were thereafter ousted ("resigned" is the polite term).

Q: Well, let's see. You were in those jobs from one to the other, for three years, weren't you?

Layton: Yes.

Q: And then you came back to Pearl as Assistant Chief of Staff to the Commander-in-Chief.

Layton: That was Admiral Stump. That was the new Joint Command, CinCPac. Up 'till that time the Commander-in-Chief Pacific had also been the CinC of the Pacific Fleet. To separate these two commands, Admiral Stump established a new Command Headquarters and turned over the job of CinC Pacific Fleet, and its Headquarters, to another Admiral. My first job was the reorganization of the intelligence division. Until this time, the same intelligence personnel (naval) worked on all problems, their results being a CinCPac, or a CinCPac Fleet estimate as the case demanded. The CinCPac staff was to be a truly joint staff - one third of the officer personnel to be from the Army, one third from the Navy and one third from the Air Force. My first task was to obtain, organize and establish the Joint Intelligence Division. CinCPac's new Headquarters were to be established in the old naval hospital at Aiea, which was being used (partially) as the Headquarters of the Fleet Marine Force, Pacific Fleet. The Marines turned over space for CinCPac Headquarters, Seabees arrived, did the conversion work in a remarkably short time, and we moved in.

At that time SEATO had been established and a SEATO intelligence conference was scheduled to be held in Singapore. Admiral Stump told me he wanted me to go as the Senior U. S. representative. I took from our Joint Intelligence Division Army, Navy and Air Force members invited a member from the Joint

Intelligence Group in Washington and a representative from CinC For Eastern Command to join us, which they did. We flew down to Sangley Point, and then to Singapore.

It was a constructive conference. It established a permanent means, by which the SEATO (which was a planningorganization) could proceed with making military and other plans based on agreed SEATO intelligence estimates. We established a modus operandus for the intelligence communities of the SEATO countries to furnish intelligence to the SEATO planners, and for periodic SEATO intelligence conferences to work up agreed estimates in response to the stated requirements of the SEATO planning group in the future.

Vietnam -- Laos, Cambodia, and North and South Vietnam were not a part of SEATO. However, there was a protocol provision by which the former French states, if they felt themselves menaced by outside aggression, could apply to, or appeal, to SEATO for assistance as might be necessary. Much later, South Vietnam did appeal to SEATO for assistance against North Vietnamese aggression.

Q: Does that take us through 1958?

Layton: Yes, after 1958, Admiral Stump called me and told me that the Air Force had been raising objections due to too many navy officers on CinCPac's Joint Staff. Here, the navy created it's own problem. Admiral Stump was the Commander-in-Chief. He had as Chief of Staff, Admiral George Anderson, The Heads of four of the five Joint Staff Divisions were Navy or Marine officers: J-1 (Joint Administration, J-2 (Joint Intelligence), J-3 (Current Plans and Operations), J-5 (Strategic Plans/War Plans). Only the J-4 Division (Joint Logistics) was not headed by a Navy or Marine officer - in this instance, an Army General headed it. The Air Force wanted either the J-3 or the J-5 Divisions to be assigned to Air Force Generals. The Navy offered the J-2 slot to them to avoid giving up the J-3 or J-5 positions.

The Air Force repeated its initial request for either the J-3 or J-5 positions instead of the offered J-2, but finally accepted it. Thus, my position was eliminated. I received orders to Washington, D. C. as Director, U. S. Naval Intelligence School. Since I had held that assignment as a Captain in 1948-50, I accepted it as the "handwriting on the wall" and began seriously to contemplate retirement.

I had known the Washington representative of the Northrop Corporation for many years as a personal friend and I saw him on several social occasions, as usual. One day he told me that the Northrop Corporation was planning to open up a new branch-office in the Far East and would want an "old Far East expert" to set it up; that since I filled these requirements, he wanted to know if I would consider retirement from the navy, if offered this job by Northrop. I replied affirmatively, subject to proper "considerations of employment." About a half year later, he telephoned me to say that the Northrop Corporation had completed its administrative actions to establish a Corporate-Branch Office in Tokyo and that my name had been approved as the new Head of of that office, subject to personal interviews and approval by the President of the Corporation and his Senior Vice Presidents. I had met some of these officials before, socially, in Washington.

The President and Chairman of the Board of Northrop, Tom Jones, notified me of their "approval" and formally offered me the position of "Director of Far Eastern Operations, Northrop International," provided I retired immediately from the Navy and joined Northrop by the first week in November 1959. I retired on 31 October 1959, flew to the West Coast the next day (Sunday) and joined Northrop the next morning 2 November. I enjoyed my employment with Northrop and have many happy memories of pleasant associations with some wonderful people. Northrop didn't preach "Loyalty Up-Loyalty Down" -- but they practiced it, much more so than the Navy did, in my opinion.

INDEX TO

REMINISCENCES

OF

REAR ADMIRAL EDWIN T. LAYTON

U. S. Navy (Retired)

U. S. Naval Institute

Annapolis, Maryland

1975

AKAGI: Japanese CV: flagship of the Task Group that attacked Pearl Harbor, p. 93.

ALEUTIAN ISLANDS: p. 150 ff.

ATTU: see Aleutians. Captured Japanese documents at Attu, p. 162-3.

CHOKAI: flagship of Japanese fleet at Savo Island, p. 134-5.

BEPPU, Kyushu, Japan: Layton chooses place as his residence while learning the Japanese language - a hot springs resort - also place of anchor for units of the Japanese fleet, p. 15.

USS BOGGS - DD: Layton becomes skipper from April 1939 to November 1940, p. 65.

USS BRAZOS: Layton boards her for passage to Dutch Harbor, p. 33-4; p. 38.

BROWN, Admiral Charles (Cat): in command of Aleutians photographic survey, p. 40.

USS CHASE: Layton's second tour of duty, p. 5-7.

CIA (Central Intelligence Agency): Agency has Permanent Chairmanship role, Intelligence Advisory Committee (nation's highest), p. 182; Layton's illustration of intelligence emphasized towards a certain policy, p. 182 ff.

CINC PAC/CINC PAC FL: Admiral Radford asks for Layton as Assistant Chief of Staff for Intelligence (Jan. 1951), p. 175; Radford names Layton as the senior U.S. representative to the Intelligence Conference of the Tripartite F.E. Command, p. 176-8.

CINC, US Fleet: Layton becomes Fleet Intelligence Officer Dec. 7, 1940, p.65 ff; Admiral Kimmel succeeds Richardson, Feb. 1941; a few diplomatic decrypted messages on Japanese activities received in Pearl Harbor, p. 69; p.74; relationship of CincUS with Combat Intelligence Unit at Pearl Harbor, p. 82-3.

COMBAT INTELLIGENCE UNIT - PEARL HARBOR: under Captain Rochefort - assigned to Commandant, 14th Naval District, p. 82-3; Rochefort's means of arriving at number of Japanese troops on various islands in the Marshalls - a major factor in decision of Nimitz to attack Kwajalein, p. 117-8; Layton's illustration of manner in which the unit developed intelligence on a given situation, p. 119-121; Midway, p. 122-123; p. 128; individual units developed by Rochefort for the various senior Task Force Commanders in the Pacific, p. 132-3; success of the Truk raid, p. 155; before battle of Midway Nimitz asks Rochefort to lay aside assigned work and concentrate on messages of Commander, Japanese First Air Fleet, p. 135-8; difficulties develop as result between Op-20 G and Rochefort, p. 135-9; Rochefort recalled to Washington, p. 138; Admiral Radford uses his special intelligence unit to nullify efforts of Japanese night aerial torpedo attacks on fleet, p. 156-7; Japanese also had radio intelligence units on their flagships, p. 157

Layton

COMMUNICATIONS INTELLIGENCE (Op 20 G): Layton assigned p. 42-3 ff; his first duties, p. 43-4 ff; the Japanese Mandated Islands, p. 44-5ff; paid no heed to diplomatic (MAGIC) messages as they pertained to Pearl Harbor and the Mandated Islands, p. 71-2; p. 82-3; Kramer's failure to pursue intercept of December 5 about barrage balloons, submarine nets, ets. at Pearl Harbor, p. 89; Layton convinced of conspiracy in Op-20 G to remove Rochefort from his job in Pearl Harbor and Layton from Nimitz staff, p. 139-40; Op-20 G misinterpretation of the Japanese code group - AF for Midway - for the West Coast of the U.S., p. 139.

COM NAV FE: Layton ordered from Com 14 (1950) to staff of Admiral Joy, p. 174; worked with others on an operation plan, p. 174.

COURTNEY, Vice Admiral Chas. E.: Director of Naval Communications, p. 42-3.

DISTRICT INTELLIGENCE OFFICER - Com 14: Layton becomes Intelligence Officer for Admiral McMorris (1950) but sent almost immediately on temporary duty as Intelligence Officer for Admiral Joy in Far East, ComNavFE, p. 174; returns from ComNavFE duties late in 1950 to Com. 14, p. 175.

DRAKE, Waldo: p. 107.

DUTCH HARBOR, Alaska: p. 33-38.

Layton

ELLICE ISLANDS: U.S. established bases there in order to obtain aerial intelligence on Tarawa and others - for eventual seizure of a position in the Marshalls, p. 116.

ENIWETOK: p. 152-3; p. 160.

FRENCH FRIGATE SHOALS: Japanese refuel their flying boats by submarine at the Shoals prior to the attack on Pearl Harbor of March 5, 1942, p. 110; Nimitz orders the Shoals mined prior to the date for Japanese assault on Midway - this prevents a Japanese reconnaissance/assault on Pearl Harbor in late May, p. 113.

FRUPAC: name given Intelligence Unit once operated by Capt. Rochefort, p. 128.

GHORMLEY, Vice Admiral Robert Lee: p. 144.

GUAM: p. 151; CincPac headquarters move to Guam in January, 1945, p. 166.

GUAM INTERCEPT STATION (Station GEORGE): p. 47; source of information on build up in Mandated Islands, p. 49-50.

HAKUYO MARU - a Japanese researcher - fisheries ship in Alaskan waters, p. 38-39.

HALSEY, Fleet Admiral Wm. F. Jr.: p. 144; p. 169.

HART, Admiral Thos. C..: conducts an official investigation of the attack on Pearl Harbor for Admiral Stark, p.98.

HARUNA - Japanese Training Ship: U.S. discovery of her actual speed after modernization, p.43-44.

HEWITT, Adm. H. Kent: Presides over the one-man investigation of the Pearl Harbor disaster by appointment of Adm. King, p.100 ff.

HOLMES, Captain W.J.: on JICPOA staff to handle intelligence for U.S. submarines, p. 163-5.

JAPAN: Layton detailed to Tokyo for language study, p. 10-11; the special method of instruction used by the Japanese instructor, p. 12-14; the Japanese capacity for revenge is underscored by the instructor, p. 14; a knowledge of Japanese thought processes, p. 14-17.

JAPANESE DEFENSE PLAN FOR EMPIRE: story of the 'old plan' as captured by the U.S., p. 158-9.

JAPANESE ESPIONAGE - West Coast: p. 28 ff; Layton designated to attend film showing before members Japanese Citizens Patriotic Society, p. 28-30; account of the film, p. 32; an incident involving an agent in Dutch Harbor, (Fleet Problem 16) p. 33-38; the HAKUTO MARU and spying for hydrographic purposes, p. 38 ff; a "narcotics" case in Seattle, p. 40-41.

JAPANESE MANDATED ISLANDS: Layton works on messages relating to them and their use by the Japanese - in Op 20 G, p. 44-45; activity in the islands stepped up in January, 1941, p. 46-47; p. 50; p. 52; p. 71; p. 84.

JAPANESE MIDSHIPMEN - on visit to San Francisco: (1925), p. 7; Layton impressed with their linguistic ability, p. 8-9; he volunteers to study Japanese language, p.10.

JAPANESE NAVAL RADIO TRAFFIC: The unusual association of aircraft, submarines, etc. prior to the March 5 attack on Pearl Harbor furnished Fleet Intelligence valued information - used later on Midway, p. 111-113; post war Japanese historians blame the aborted reconnaissance/bombing attack on Pearl Harbor (late May, 1942) as reason for failure at Midway, p. 113.

JAPANESE NAVAL SHIPS: Major units in attack on Pearl Harbor (Dec. 7, 1941), p. 93-4; major units for proposed attack on Port Moresby, p. 120-121.

JAPANESE SURRENDER: Adm. Nimitz takes Layton to Japan for ceremony - Layton acts as body guard, p. 168

JICPOA: see entries under Combat Intelligence Unit, Nimitz, Rochefort, Layton: Organization of JICPOA, p. 128-9; Layton recommends Col. Jos. J. Twitty, Corps of Engineers, USA as new head of JICPOA - he serves throughout the war, p. 129; Layton gives an illustration of effectiveness of Combat Intelligence on Saipan, p. 130; Capt. Holmes joins staff to handle intercept intelligence for U.S. submarines, p. 163-5.

JOHNSON, The Hon. Nelson T.: U.S. Minister in Peiping (1932), p. 17; p. 21.

KAMAKURA, Japan: Historic Japanese city - never bombed by U.S. - p. 169; visited by Adm. Nimitz on day of surrender, p. 169-70.

KIMMEL, RADM Husband E.: briefed by Layton on significance of Japanese build-up in the Mandated Islands when he took over command from Adm. J.O. Richardson, p. 47; p. 68; raises question with Adm. Stark (June 1941) about Japanese activities in the Mandated Islands, p. 48-50; p. 53; Layton says he was not furnished several very significant decrypts from

Washington on Pearl Harbor p. 69; p. 71; Layton had translated parts of a Japanese book - "Shall America and Japan fight?" - contained pertinent information for the Cinc, U S Fleet, p. 72-3; asks Capt. McMorris for his reaction to a possible Japanese attack on Pearl Harbor, p. 73-4; on Dec. 6 asks Adm. Pye for reaction to news Japanese were moving towards the Gulf of Siam, p. 74-5; asks ONI for more diplomatic intercepts in late 1941, p. 76-77; p. 78; p. 80; p. 82; on Dec1. 1941 asks for report on location of Japanese fleet units, p. 87-88; distressed at lack of information on Japanese carrier locations - his statement about possibility of carriers coming around Diamond Head, p. 87-88; p. 90; p. 92-3; slightly wounded by spent machine gun bullet during Pearl Harbor raid, p. 95; Layton says Kimmel had left Pearl Harbor by time Nimitz took over, p. 96-7; Layton's story of the Court of Inquiry on Pearl Harbor - and the subsequent one man investigation, p. 97-104; p. 126-7.

KING, Fleet Admiral Ernest J.: as COMINCH he ordered a one-man investigation of Pearl Harbor following the special Navy Court of Inquiry that had failed to blame Adm. Kimmel for the disaster, p. 100; Layton's opinions of his actions in the Pearl Harbor investigation, p. 103-4; his involvement in the recall of Capt. Rochefort, p. 138-143; p. 152.

KISKA: See entry under Aleutians.

KITTS, Vice Admiral Wm.A. III (Bill): p. 75-6,

KOGA, Fleet Admiral M. (Japanese) Commander in Chief of the Combined Japanese Fleet, p. 159.

KWAJALEIN: see entries under MARSHALL ISLANDS.

    p. 117 ff; p. 145-8; p. 152-3; the fortunate capture of Japanese document showing location of mine fields in Mandated Islands, p. 162-3.

KORYAKU BUTAI: used in despatches dealing with Japanese preparations for invasion of Port Moresby, p. 120; Japanese words for 'invasion assault force' - messages using this term and identifying Japanese objective as AF were interpreted correctly in Pearl Harbor as Midway, p. 122.

LAYTON, Rear Admiral Edwin T.: Personal data, p. 1-4; volunteers for Japanese language study, p. 9-10; his personal reactions to developments before Pearl Harbor attack, p. 74-75; Capt. Kitts and the "Saturday crisis", p. 75-6; his relations with Admiral Kinnel, p. 78; his liaison with Combat Intelligence Unite at Pearl Harbor, p. 83-4; his experiences with the 'trial' lawyer at the Hewitt one-man investigation of Pearl Harbor, p. 100 ff; CNO Nimitz advises Layton to apply for Special Duty Only (Intelligence) - he accepted in mid 1948 - assigned to direct the new Intelligence School in Washington, p. 173; makes Flag Rank (June, 1953) - becomes Deputy Director of Intelligence, JCS, p. 181-2; named as J.2 (Intelligence) on staff of Adm. Stump (CincPac), p. 189 ff;

returns to Washington as Director (2nd time) of U. S. Navy Intelligence School (1959) - resigns from Navy, Oct. 31, 1959 - goes with Northrop Corporation to head new branch office in Tokyo, p. 191-2.

LOCKWOOD, Vice Admiral Charles A.: investigates the defective torpedoes at request of Adm. Nimitz, p. 165-6.

MacArthur, General Douglas: p. 168.

MAGIC: The diplomatic decrypts referred to as MAGIC at the Pearl Harbor hearings, p. 71; FDR orders "purple" cypher machine intended for Rochefort in Pearl Harbor to be handed over to the British, p. 71; Layton sees failure to provide Magic Machine for Pearl Harbor as one of the significant steps leading to the disaster, p. 80-82; MAGIC message (furnished P.H.) in early December outlining Japanese strategy for enticing British from Malaya into Siam, p. 85-6.

MAJURO (Marshall Islands): see entries under MARSHALL ISLANDS, ADMIRAL NIMITZ, KWAJALEIN.

MANCHURIA: pp. 21-27; Layton sent to Harbin with message from Minister Johnson, p. 21; stops in Dairen - visits Port Arthur naval base, gathers data, p. 22-23; Layton in Harbin, p. 23 ff; first hand knowledge of Japanese preparations, p. 24-25; visit to Shan hai Kwan, p. 26-27.

MARIANA ISLANDS: importance to the Japanese in defense of the mainland, p. 158 ff.

MARSHALL ISLANDS: as a result of Pearl Harbor attack the U.S. Navy delayed implementation of a plan to obtain a base in the Marshall Islands - and caused setting up of Intelligence

Center at Pearl Harbor, p. 114-5; after capture of Tarawa Layton's intelligence on the Marshalls increased; he advised Nimitz daily on Japanese efforts to take equipment, men, naval units from Kwajalein (the headquarters island) to perimeter islands less strongly fortified, p. 117; p. 145-7; p. 152-4; p. 158-60.

McCOLLUM, RADM Arthur: Layton requests more diplomatic intercepts for Adm. Kimmel - request turned down, p. 76-77.

McCORMICK, Admiral Lynde D.: head of War Plans on staff of CincPac (May, 1942) - Nimitz delegates him to examine Combat Intelligence traffic analysis pertaining to Midway, p. 123-4.

McMORRIS, Vice Admiral (Sock) Charles H.: his opinion on a possible Japanese attack on Pearl Harbor, p. 73-4; p. 76.

MERCER, RADM Preston V.: suggested to Admiral Nimitz that briefings and staff conferences of CincPac be taped, p. 150.

MIDWAY: the exact date set by the Japanese for attack is determined, p. 108-9; ff; Japanese traffic analysis (May, 1942) indicates Midway as the objective, p. 122-5; Layton denies all written stories that Nimitz had the entire Japanese battle order before Midway, p. 125-7; p. 137-8; p. 155.

MILI (Marshall Islands): see entries under MARSHALL ISLANDS, ADMIRAL NIMITZ, KWAJALEIN.

MITSCHER, Admiral Marc Andrew: p. 155; p. 158; p. 160.

MIZUHO - Japanese Seaplane Carrier: sunk by U.S. submarine off Tokyo Bay, p. 164.

LAYTON

N.A. Tokyo (Naval Attache): Layton assigned as Assistant Naval Attache (Apr. 1937 - March 1939), p. 55 ff; Layton offers assistance to the former Russian Naval Attache (in Washington) who had difficulties with the Japanese immigration people, p. 55-56; the Russians reciprocate, p. 57-8; relations with Admiral Yamamoto, p. 57-8; the request for Japanese aid in the search for Amelia Earhart, p. 57, p. 61; evidence of Japanese militarism in Tokyo and elsewhere, p. 62-3; Layton visits Shanghai, p.63; the Japanese handling of the report that they were building huge BBs, p. 63-5.

NAVAL INTELLIGENCE SCHOOL: Established in Washington, D.C.,1948 - Layton becomes Director, p. 173; Layton returns as Director in 1959 after CincPac assignment - p. 191-2.

NIMITZ, Fleet Admiral Chester W.: Layton asks to be detached when he takes over Pacific Command from Adm. Pye - Nimitz refuses and asks Layton to "be the Admiral Nagumo" on his staff - to think Japanese, etc., p. 79-80; p. 96-7; p. 107; Layton's relations and access to the CincPac, p. 108-9; Nimitz and traffic analysis, p. 109; p. 111; reason for his decision to attack Kwajalein in the Marshalls, p. 117-8; Midway preparations, p.122-125; Nimitz unwilling to build a larger staff at CincPac, p. 127-8; later authorizes establishment of Intelligence Center attached to 14th Naval District - this in turn becomes J.I.C.P.O.A., p. 128; he asks Rochefort to devote his time to messages from Japanese Commander, First Air Fleet in period immediately before Midway, p. 136-8; unsuccessful in his efforts to

retain Rochefort in Pearl Harbor or to get him a DSM,
p. 138-141; Nimitz and the assault on Kwajalein, p. 145-7;
p. 50 (on taping staff conferences); his use of captured
defense plan of the Japanese, p. 160-1; investigates
defective torpedoes at outset of war, p. 165-6; intends
that Layton accompany Adm. Sherman to Manila for preliminary talks on Japanese surrender, p. 166-7; takes Layton to
Japan for surrender - a day of sightseeing after ceremony,
p. 168-170; Layton feels Nimitz would be a more likely
target for Japanese assassin than would Gen. MacArthur,
p. 168-9; detached from duties as CincPac - goes to Washington as CNO, p. 171; Nimitz advises Layton to apply for
Special Duty (Intelligence) - Layton is accepted in mid
1948, p. 172-3.

NORTHROP CORPORATION: Layton resigns from Navy, joins Northrop on November 1, 1959 - to head Far East Office, p. 191-2.

ONI (Office of Naval Intelligence): Layton returns to ONI (1933) - begins work on plotting of strategic Japanese industrial sites, p. 27; assigned to Op 20 G (June, 1936) - Communications Intelligence, p. 41-2; Layton addressed Comdr. Arthur McCollum in late 1941 asking for diplomatic decrypts for benefit of Admiral Kimmel - McCollum turns down request, p. 76-77.

ONI Manual: p. 53-4; p. 77.

PEARL HARBOR: see entries under Pearl Harbor Investigations; Admiral Nimitz; Communications Intelligence; Adm. Kimmel; MAGIC messages pertaining to Pearl Harbor, p. 71; questions raised in Japanese book - "Shall America and Japan Fight?", p. 72; Kimmel very much interested, p. 73; Japanese spies in Hawaii, p. 78; p. 80. Layton's account of events on Dec. 7, 1941, p. 90-5; the second attack by the Japanese (March 5, 1942) - two Japanese seaplanes, p. 110-111; the value of an analysis of Japanese naval radio traffic, p. 112-113; one good result of Japanese attack - delay in the U.S. assault on the Marshall Islands and the setting up of the Intelligence Center at Pearl Harbor, p. 114-5.

PEARL HARBOR INVESTIGATION: Layton forbidden to use despatch on Mandated Islands before the Joint Congressional Investigation of Pearl Harbor, p.52 ff; p.73-4; p. 76-79; p.80; p..82; p.85; p. 89; Layton's story of the Naval Court of Inquiry, the findings, the new one-man investigation and ultimate putting of blame on Admiral Kimmel and General Short, p. 98-104; Layton called before the Joint Congressional Committee (Feb. 1946), p. 171-2.

PEIPING (Peking): Layton ordered to the Legation (1932) for duty as Assistant Naval Attache - duty under direction of Comdr. Cleveland McCauley, the Naval Attache, p. 17 ff; detailed to communicate directly with the Japanese Legation Guard, p. 19 ff; Layton works with Chinese Intelligence on the movements of the Japanese Legation Guard, p. 19-20.

PORT MORESBY: Layton uses the Japanese proposed attack on Port Moresby as illustration of how intelligence was developed at Pearl Harbor, p. 119-121.

PYE, Vice Admiral Wm. S.: in command of Battle Force - on USS CALIFORNIA, p. 74-5; his appearance during the attack on Pearl Harbor, p. 94-5; his timid approach to command after Pearl Harbor - his recall of the expedition for the relief of Wake Island, p. 105-6.

USS PENNSYLVANIA: Layton ordered to her (1933) for duty - wins the Navy E. for 14 inch turret competition - Commendation, p. 28; Layton named Cinc's boarding officer on all Japanese naval ships calling in San Pedro harbor, p. 28; p. 33; p. 40.

PULESTON, Captain Wm. Dilworth: Director of Naval Intelligence, p. 42.

RADFORD, Admiral Arthur W.: uses the information from his Combat Intelligence Unit to nullify Japanese night aerial torpedo attacks on fleet units, p. 156-7; as CincPac/Cinc Pac Fl asks Layton to join his staff as Intelligence Officer- p. 175; Names Layton as U.S. Representative to Tripartite Intelligence Conferences - his arrangements for transportation of British and French delegates to Hawaii fall through, p. 177-8; Radford takes Layton back to Washington when he becomes Chairman of the JCS, p. 180-1; Layton promoted to Flag Rand (SDO Intelligence), June, 1953 - becomes Deputy Director for Intelligence, JCS, p. 181-2.

REEVES, Admiral Jos. Mason: Cinc. U.S. Fleet, p.28, p.33.

RICHARDSON, Admiral James O.: Cinc US Fleet - Layton joins his staff in Dec. 1940, p. 45; sees significance in messages about Japanese build-up in the Mandated Islands, p. 47. asks Layton to become Fleet Intelligence officer on his staff (Dec. 7, 1940), p. 65 ff; Layton acts as aide to Japanese Admiral Nomura during his brief visit to Hawaii - at Richardson's request, p. 66-67.

ROCHEFORT, Captain Jos. J. USN (ret): sent to Japan at same time as Layton for language study, p. 10; Intelligence Officer on staff of Admiral Jos. Mason Reeves (1933), p. 28-29; sends Layton to Dutch Harbor on an espionage mission, p. 33 ff; Layton confers with him in Jan. 1941- Rochefort then head of the Communications Intelligence Unit at Pearl Harbor- p. 45-6; his office at Pearl Harbor involved before Dec.7, 1941 with cipher and code recovery for a Japanese naval system - also a daily Japanese naval traffic analysis for benefit of Admiral Kimmel, p.70; Rochefort did not see the "Magic" (diplomatic decrypts) that went to Cavite and the British, p. 71; His Communications Intelligence Unit was under Commandant, 14th Naval District, p. 82; Layton had active liaison with him on behalf of the CincPacFleet, p. 83; p. 83-5; his daily Japanese naval radio traffic analysis reports, p. 86-7; p. 90; p. 93; informs Admiral Nimitz of date set by Japanese for attack on Midway, p. 108-9; more on traffic analysis before Midway, p. 122-24; traffic analysis prior to battle of Coral Sea, p. 119-121; FRUPAC, new name given Richefort Intelligence Unit, p. 128; Rochefort organizes special combat Intelligence Units for operating with senior Task Force Commanders in Pacific, p. 132-3; Nimitz orders Rochefort to lay aside assigned work from Washington and concentrate on messages from Commander, Japanese First Air Fleet, p. 135-8; difficulties develop between Op. 20G and Rochefort, p. 135-9; recalled to Washington - his DSM cancelled, p. 138, p. 140-1; a yoeman sent from Washington to gather data on Rochefort and Layton, p. 141-3; see entries also under: Combat Intelligence, the Marshall Islands, Admiral King, Admiral Nimitz.

ROOSEVELT: The Hon. Franklin D. - President of the U.S.: Layton's opinion that the decision of FDR to turn over the MAGIC machine (intended for Pearl Harbor) to the British was a real factor leading to disaster of Pearl Harbor, p. 80-81; informed of the MAGIC messages of December 6, p. 81-82; his prestige involved in placing blame for Pearl Harbor, p. 99; his apparent wishes to "white wash" Washington for the P.H. disaster, p. 103.

SAFFORD, Capt. Lawrence F.: head of Op-20 G when Layton worked there prior to WW II - Lt. Wenger the actual executive, p. 43; p. 125; p. 136.

SAVO ISLAND: Layton reconstructs the developing battle as it might have been should Turner have accepted a Combat Intelligence Unit, p. 134-5.

SEATO: p. 178, p. 189-190

SHERMAN, Admiral Forrest P.: p. 147 Adm. Nimitz sends him as his representative to Manila in August, 1945 to discuss preliminaries to Japanese surrender - fails to take Layton as requested - Nimitz angry, p. 166-7.

SHIMIZU: Japanese agent resident in Dutch Harbor, Alaska, p. 35-38.

SHORT, Lt. Gen. Walter C.: Commanding General in Hawaii at time of Pearl Harbor attack, - the Army Court of Inquiry and the one man investigation that followed, p. 98-104.

SMITH, General H.M. (Howling Mad), USMC: p. 118; p. 148-9; p. 153; he pays his bet on Majuro, p. 153-4.

SONNETT, Lt. Comdr. John Francis (USNR): Acted as Counsel (prosecuting attorney, says Layton) for Admiral Hewitt in the one-man investigation of Pearl Harbor, p. 100 ff.

SPRUANCE, Admiral Raymond: p. 118; p. 132; p. 148-9; Layton assigns reason for Spruance's caution during the invasion of Saipan, p. 161.

STARK, Admiral Harold R.: As CNO, Kimmel confers with him in Washington, June 1941 p. 48; p. 50; p. 77; p. 81; the Pearl Harbor Courts of Inquiry, p. 94-104.

STUMP, Admiral Felix: Layton returns to Pearl Harbor as Assistant Chief of Staff to Stump- reorganizes the Intelligence Division, p. 189; sends Layton to SEATO Intelligence Conference, p. 189-190; Air Force asks for greater representation on CincPac Staff - Stump gives them J.2 (Intelligence) and Layton returns to Washington as Director of the U.S. Naval Intelligence School - sees it as his last assignment, p. 191.

TARAWA (Gilbert Islands): an early objective of the U.S. fleet, p. 116-117.

USS TARBELL: Layton ordered to her at Dutch Harbor in connection with Japanese spying for hydrographic purposes, p. 38 ff.

TAROA: (Marshall Islands): see entries under MARSHALL ISLANDS ADMIRAL NIMITZ, KWAJALEIN.

TIBURON, California: location of the Naval Net Depot - Layton goes there in command, 1946, p. 171.

TORPEDOES: defective U.S. torp does at beginning of World War II, p. 165-6.

TRANS-SIBERIAN Railroad: p. 183-188; see also entry under CIA.

TRIPARTITE INTELLIGENCE CONFERENCES: Set up on six-month basis (1951) by the U.S., British and French Commanders in the Far East, p. 176 ff; came under SEATO when that organization was set up, p. 178.

TRUK: Carrier Task Force raid, February, 1943, p. 154-5.

TURNER, Admiral R. Kelly: misunderstood the fact that Kimmel was <u>not</u> receiving the diplomatic decrypts from Washington, p. 80; p. 118; p. 130-1; p. 134-5; p. 146; p. 162.

TWITTY, Brig. General Jos. J. Twitty: Corps of Engineers, USA- becomes head of JICPOA (J-2 on staff of CincPac) and serves throughout the Pacific War, p. 129.

VIET Nam (INdo-China): p. 177-179; Layton guest of the French Commander - tours battle area in the Hanoi area against the Viet Minh, p. 179-80.

WAKE ISLAND: Adm. Pye and the expedition for the relief of Wake Island, p. 105-6.

WE address system - Japanese Navy: p. 45-6; information gleaned by Layton from intercepts, p. 84.

WENGER, RADM Jos. N.: Op 20 G under Safford, p. 43.

USS WEST VIRGINIA: Layton's first tour of duty on her, p. 4-5; plays host to Japanese Midshipmen's Training Squadrom in San Francisco (1925), p. 7-8; Layton impressed with linguistic ability of the Japanese midshipmen, p. 7-8.

WOTJE (Marshall Islands): see entries under MARSHALL ISLANDS, ADMIRAL NIMITZ, KWAJALEIN.

YAMAMOTO, Fleet Admiral I.: Japanese Cinc - Layton's relations with him in Tokyo before WW II - an estimate of the man, p. 58-59; Layton's advice to Admiral Nimitz on the possible intercept of the Yamamoto plane in the South Pacific, p. 59-61; p. 154.

www.ingramcontent.com/pod-product-compliance
Lightning Source LLC
Chambersburg PA
CBHW080613170426
43209CB00007B/1421